FLOWER CRAFTS

FLOWER CRAFTS

Emma Wood with Jane Merer

ORBIS PUBLISHING · London

Acknowledgments
The publishers are grateful to Maureen Jones, who
designed and made all the projects in the book, with the
exception of the following:
Fresh and dried flower arrangements by Jenny Raworth,
St Margarets, Twickenham
Painted flowers by Jane Merer
Poppy cushion by Gwynne Jones
Stencil designs on pages 46–51 by Lyn le Grice
Stencilled bag on page 55 by Sue Storey
Paper flowers on pages 74–5 by Vera Jeffrey
Fabric flowers by Julia Marafie

© 1982 by Orbis Publishing Limited, London
First published in Great Britain by Orbis Publishing
Limited, London 1982

Printed in Italy

ISBN 0-85613-330-2

Contents

Fresh flowers

The practice of using fresh flowers as decorations is a very ancient one; and since time immemorial people have been celebrating festivals of all kinds with flowers and plants, not only adorning their homes with them but wearing them as well. A wedding is the perfect occasion for sumptuous displays of flowers on a grand scale. For a bold and festive pedestal display (left), large flowers in light colours, built up into a simple shape with strong lines, are more effective than intricate detail and sombre colours, which would be lost when viewed from a distance, especially in the dim light of a church. Such an arrangement needs plenty of foliage to give it depth and mass: use both green and silver leaves, tall grasses and flowers such as *Molucella* to add height, and ferns and other trailing material to hang below the level of the container, hiding it completely.

Instructions for making other festive flower arrangements are also given in this chapter. Detailed information on the selection and preparation of fresh flowers and on the equipment needed to arrange them is included too so that, whatever the occasion and setting, you will be able to make the most of your flowers, ensuring that they look their best.

The description overleaf of the way a flower is constructed is designed to help you not only in this chapter but throughout the book: skill in all flowercrafts will be increased by a knowledge of fresh flowers as well as by an enthusiasm for using them, whether fresh, dried, or pressed, or as a motif in many other crafts.

7

Parts of a flower

The parts shown in this cross-section of a typical flower (right) are described below. Refer to the diagram not only when using fresh flowers but also for the other flowercrafts described in this book, particularly the paper and fabric flowers.

The corolla of petals is the most showy and easily recognizable part of most flowers. This is surrounded in the bud stage by the circular calyx, which protects the flower before it opens and is composed of leaf-like sepals, which turn back to form a decorative frill round the open petals. The pistil is the central, female part of the flower, and is made up of the stigma which receives the pollen, the style through which the pollen passes, and the ovary at its base containing the immature seeds. The stamens, which vary in number from one to hundreds, are the male part of the flower, and comprise anthers, the tips which contain the pollen, and fine stalks, called filaments, by which the anthers are attached to the flower.

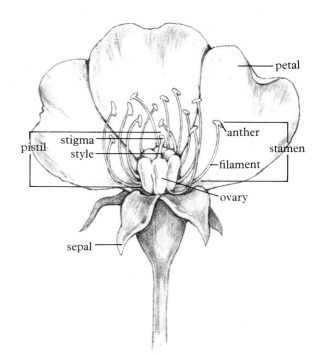

Tools & materials

Containers Two sorts of container are needed for fresh flowers: those for conditioning the cut flowers before use, such as buckets; and those for displaying the flowers in arrangements. Vases come in all shapes and sizes, the most useful being a tall, narrow jar or jug, a shallow bowl, and a rounded shape with narrow neck. The shape chosen will obviously depend on the form and function of a display, and need not be an actual vase: everyday objects such as casserole dishes and glasses can be used.

Cutters The best tool for cutting most flowers is a pair of florist's stub scissors with a serrated edge, which cut cleanly and are easy to handle. A pair of ordinary sharp scissors can be used instead for thin-stemmed plants, but for woody stems such as those of roses and hydrangeas, secateurs should be used. A sharp pruning knife or pruning shears will be required for thicker branches.

Wire Stub wire and silver reel wire, available from florists, are the main types of wire needed for floral decorations. Stub wire, used to strengthen or replace stems, comes in eight precut lengths and several diameters, from 0.20 mm (3.6 gauge) to 1.25 mm (18 gauge). A medium weight suits most flowers. The finer, more pliable silver reel wire is used to bind wired flowers to each other and in general assembly; and fuse wire can be used for the same purpose.

Tape Coloured florist's tape, also called gutta-percha, is used to conceal external wiring. Simply wind the tape round the stem: glue is not required as the tape is self-adhesive.

Florist's foam Commonly known by one of the most popular brand names – Oasis – this plastic, dense sponge-like material comes in hard square or round blocks which can be cut to size with a knife, and is used to support the stems of plants in a display. The foam is soaked in water for an hour or so until saturated, then the stems are inserted into it – they should pierce the foam easily, although you may have to make the holes with a skewer for very delicate stems. When fitting the foam into its container, make sure that there is enough room round the sides of it for more water to be added daily to keep the foam moist. One piece of foam can be used several times (store damp in a sealed plastic bag).

Pinholders There are many types and sizes of pinholder available, all consisting of numerous fine prongs embedded in a heavy base. They are very useful for supporting all kinds of flower display, particularly in shallow containers, as they can easily be disguised by plant material. Their weight adds stability to a tall or top-heavy arrangement. Stems are simply pushed down on the prongs vertically, then bent into position.

Chicken wire This light wire netting can be used alone to support flowers, or with foam or a pinholder. Use enough 50 mm (2 in) mesh wire to fill the container when loosely crumpled.

Adhesive tape Masking tape is another useful means of support for some flower arrangements, criss-crossed over the rim of a container, and is also useful for taping together flowers for bouquets and buttonholes.

Adhesive clay (such as Oasis Fix) This can be used for anchoring container arrangements if they are at all unstable or likely to be knocked, and also for securing foam or a pinholder to the bottom of a container.

Choosing fresh flowers

Certain flowers lend themselves perfectly to the arranger's art – carnations, mimosa, narcissi and roses all spring immediately to mind – but every plant can be used in some way for fresh flower arrangements. The effects which can be achieved obviously depend on what is available just as much as on the skill of the arranger and the style of the arrangement being made, but, with a little planning, fresh plant material can be gathered from the garden virtually all year round.

Wild flowers have a special appeal: there is something particularly attractive about the first spring primroses or bluebells, as reminders of a woodland walk. It is illegal, however, to take flowers from other people's land without permission, and many wild species are now protected by law to ensure their survival. Choose only plants which are in abundance, don't uproot them, and don't pick them at all if they are likely to die before you reach home.

If you are buying flowers from a florist, look for a shop where all the plants are in good condition and cut flowers are kept standing in deep water. Choose flowers in bud or only partly open, to ensure their long life in a warmer atmosphere. The foliage should also be healthy and undamaged. Put them in water as soon as you possibly can.

Picking flowers

If possible, pick flowers in fairly dry, calm weather, so that they are not spoiled by wind and rain. Cool, cloudy days are best: the most important thing to remember when picking is that the flowers must not be kept short of water, and sunshine draws the moisture out of the flowers, which makes them liable to wilt more quickly when picked. Even so, the flowers will need conditioning for a few hours before use (see below), so pick them well before you need them. On hot days, gather them either early in the morning before the sun is up, so that the flowers have benefited from the cool of the night, or in the evening when their food reserves are highest and they can be conditioned overnight.

Examine the plant carefully before you pick, to make sure that it is at its best. To avoid the disappointment of fast-wilting arrangements, make sure that it is at the right stage of its life-cycle for cutting – some plants never come out fully in water if taken too early, while mature blooms which are already full of pollen may not last very long indoors. Most flowers, including poppies, peonies, roses, phlox, irises and shrub flowers, are best cut when the buds are just beginning to unfold, whereas some, such as chrysanthemums and dahlias, should be fully out, though still with firm centres. All types of daisy last longest if picked with firm green centres with only a little pollen on them. Contrary to the general rule, however, mimosa looks best near the end of its days, when it is full of pollen.

Cutting and transporting All plants should be cleanly cut when picked, rather than torn or broken off the plant. Not only does this prevent damage to the parent plant but it enables the cut flower to take up water more easily, and therefore last longer in an arrangement. Stub scissors are the best tool to use for most flowers (see Tools & materials).

Ideally you should have a deep container full of water, even several of them, with you when cutting flowers from the garden. Take a good length of stem with each flower or piece of foliage, and cut each stem at an angle, to expose as large a surface as possible to the water and to prevent the stem ends resting squarely on the bottom of the container (which they would do if cut straight across). These measures facilitate water absorption.

Strip away any unnecessary foliage from the base of the stem, being careful not to take off too much initially, then plunge the stems in water immediately. Leave the containers in a shady place while you cut more flowers.

The above applies equally to wild flowers, though of course, it is usually not possible to have a container of water with you. Nor is it easy to transport flowers far in water, although many competition flower arrangers use wooden racks to hold water containers while travelling by car. An alternative for small flowers is to take a plastic bag containing damp tissue paper or cotton wool, and to put the flowers in them as soon as you pick them, sealing the bag to retain the moisture. Larger plants should be wrapped in moist tissue paper or newspaper inside large plastic bags. If you are travelling a long distance, use a houseplant spray to refresh the plants from time to time.

Preparation and conditioning

To keep them alive as long as possible, cut flowers should be allowed to absorb as much water as they can as soon as they are picked. In general, all flowers should first be put in containers of tepid water deep enough to cover the whole length of the stems. Foliage can also be immersed, but not the flower-heads. Tap water is perfectly acceptable, and needs no additives to counteract bacteria if the containers are kept thoroughly clean. Some plants benefit from soaking in even warmer water, including those with tough or woody stems such as roses, chrysanthemums and carnations.

Flowers which have been away from water for

The type of container you choose for a flower arrangement should depend very much on the overall effect you wish to achieve; its shape, size and the material from which it is made should determine the type of plants that are used, their colours and whether they are wired or not, and also the methods used to support them in the container. For example, the jug used here (left) is tall and narrow enough to be able to support the stems of the flowers without any foam, chicken wire or pinholder being necessary. This gives the flowers an informal look, and the style of arrangement also suits the colourful mixture of blooms and foliage, which includes privet, *Senecio*, ferns, daisy chrysanthemums, nerines, pinks and gypsophila.

A small flower arrangement suitable for a breakfast tray or table setting, like the one shown above, is very easy to make. All you need is a ramekin dish or similar and a block of florist's foam cut to fit the dish so that it protrudes just beyond the rim. No wiring of the plants is required: simply push sprays of greenery and small flowers on quite short stems into the top and sides of the wet foam until no foam is visible and the arrangement looks pleasing from all angles. Using foam means that each stem can be precisely placed, and stops the flowers moving, a boon in situations where the flowers might be knocked.

more than a few minutes should have their stems recut, again at an angle, before being conditioned in water. This is to break any seal that might have formed at the end of the stem.

Hard, woody or tough stems should also have their ends crushed with a small hammer or mallet. Any bark should be peeled off at the end of the stem before the stems are crushed. Stems which exude a sticky or milky liquid should have their ends either held in boiling water for thirty seconds or burnt with a flame until blackened, in order to break the seal formed by the fluid as it hardens on contact with air. Floppy stems such as those of tulips can be made more rigid if they are wrapped in stiff paper and held upright while being conditioned in water, while hollow stems can be made to last longer if they are filled with water (hold the flowers upside down and pour water into them) and their ends plugged with cotton wool.

No matter how many times the stems are recut for an arrangement or display, they should be given the appropriate treatment each time as described above, if they are to be long-lasting.

Arranging flowers

Choose flowers for arrangements according to the season, the occasion, and a specific plan. Formal displays, say for a dinner party or a wedding, will demand certain types of flower and foliage, while less formal ones will need others; and the room setting and its colour scheme must also be taken into account. Unless you are creating a strictly formal or symmetrical arrangement, perhaps to decorate a church or an impressive entrance hall, it is best to keep the flowers as natural as possible to give a spontaneous rather than a contrived effect, and this means relying as little as possible on wiring, if at all.

Always fit the arrangement to its situation, so that, for instance, it does not hide a picture on the wall behind it, or dominate a dinner table so that the diners cannot see each other. For this reason it helps if you can work in a similar space and surroundings, looking down on long, low arrangements and perhaps improvising a turntable for circular arrangements which will be seen from all sides.

A sense of proportion is possibly the most important factor in a successful arrangement and, to achieve this, a balance of colour, shape and size, in both plant material and container, must be attained. Do not adhere rigidly to rules of display, but bear in mind the precept that an arrangement should be at least one and a half times as tall as its container. For

a traditional arrangement, first define the outline
(1), then add major blooms and leaves at the centre
(2) and work outwards from them, keeping the
arrangement flowing and gradually leaning the
lower flowers forward more (3). Avoid
overcrowding and crossing stems, and do not use
big leaves at the apex of an arrangement, but keep
the main mass and bulk of it at its base. Make sure
that the shapes and colours of materials do not clash:
for example, hot colours such as orange are less
successful with cool colours – say, pale green – than
with other hot colours such as yellow or red; while
the severe, strong shapes of laurel leaves or gladioli
would not be appropriate with more delicate flowers
like nigella or sweet peas.

Containers

Glass and china vases are by no means the only
containers suitable for flower display – whatever is
to hand can be used, as long as it suits the flowers.
The arrangement should not be too tall or massive
for its container, nor too short that the container
predominates.

Choose pots and jars in neutral shades and rough
textures to complement simple bark and foliage;
and for a peaceful, serene effect avoid bright
primary colours and stick to cool greens and blues.
White is particularly useful, since it goes with every
colour, and can help pull together several strong
colours in an arrangement.

If you have some old china which is too fragile to
be in general use, or not watertight, you can still use
it for flower displays. Either put a piece of wet
florist's foam in a plastic bag and fit this into the
container, inserting the flowers in the foam, or use
little pots or jam jars inside the container. Baskets
can also be used in this way.

Foam will support all kinds of arrangement and is
very easy to use. It can be enclosed in a layer of
chicken wire for extra support in very large or
heavy displays. It should always extend well beyond
the rim of the container so the stems can be inserted
into its sides (4). Crumpled chicken wire (5) and
pinholders (6) are also essential means of support
for many kinds of flower display, especially in wide
or shallow bowls (see Tools & materials, page 8),
but you will need to experiment with them to know
which is best for a particular purpose, and which
you prefer using.

Wiring

Whereas flowers in most container arrangements
need to look as natural as possible, flowers which
are to be worn or held – in bouquets, buttonholes
and head-dresses – must usually have some form of

wire support if they are to remain looking good over a reasonable length of time.

One of the simplest forms of wiring, which can be used to good effect in some arrangements also, is to push a stub wire as far as possible up the stem of a heavy-headed flower. Flowers with hollow stems and thick centres can also be strengthened by means of a stub wire: bend one end into a small hook and insert the other end into the centre of the flower-head and down into the stem, embedding the hook in the flower itself. (These methods are shown in figures 2 and 3 on page 25.) Choose a wire of a weight and length to correspond to the type of stem and flower.

Other stems benefit from being cut very short and wired externally. These include brittle, fine or damaged stems, and flowers to be used together in a large bouquet, where their overall weight can be lessened by removing most of the stem from each flower. For a flower to look as natural as possible, leave about 50 mm (2 in) of stem. For a solid, firm stem, simply insert a wire through it from the bottom up to the flower-head, but for a softer, fleshier stem insert the wire sideways through the base of the flower-head (1), pull it through and bend the ends down until parallel with the stem, then twist them together in wide loops (2) before binding with tape.

Crosswiring is used when all the stem has been discarded. Push two light wires at right angles through the base of the flower-head (3), bend them down and twist them round each other to form a false stem (4). This is the method generally used for wiring pinks and carnations for bouquets, and is useful for preventing buds from opening.

Another wiring method, particularly useful for foliage, flowers too fragile for piercing, or for a large bouquet, does not involve inserting the wire into the plant. Instead, one end of a stub wire is bent into a hairpin-shaped hook about 25 mm (1 in) long, and this is placed over the stem or stems with the hook at the top (5). The long end of the wire is then twisted round the short end and the stem(s), and brought down to continue the stem (6), before being taped. To support even heavier materials, bend the wire into two equal halves, place it against the stem as before, then twist one half round the other a few times before bringing them both down straight, to form a stem (7).

Although many leaves are rigid enough not to need wiring, others may need support, particularly if they are being worn. Small leaves can have fine wire threaded along their midribs, with one end of it wound round the leaf stem to form a new, longer stem (8), or they can be wired in one of the other ways already described.

13

The graceful symmetry of a bride's bouquet is complemented by a pretty bridesmaid's posy (left). The bouquet has lilies, ivy, freesias and gypsophila; the posy has *Senecio*, rosemary, chrysanthemums, nerines and carnations.

A bridesmaid's head-dress (below) is not difficult to make using wired flowers (instructions on page 16).

For a wedding buttonhole or corsage (bottom) choose suitable flowers – orchids for the bride's mother, carnations for the ushers – and wire as described on page 13. Attach foliage such as ferns to the main bloom(s) with fine wire, then cover the stems with tape, binding in a safety pin placed along the stem.

Bridesmaids' posies

Informal posies

Small, round, slightly domed bouquets, often finished with a frill of lace, are particularly popular for informal, country weddings and for small bridesmaids. The style of these is most suitable for simple, less exotic flowers, such as primroses, forget-me-nots, pansies and cornflowers, as well as the more conventional rosebuds, carnations, lily-of-the-valley, gypsophila and mimosa. Evergreen foliage is useful too, particularly ivy, and so are flowers with a greenish hue such as *Alchemilla mollis*. Silver foliage – *Senecio* and *Santolina*, for example – mingles well in informal arrangements, and for a more unusual, perfumed posy, sprigs of lavender and rosemary can also be included.

Informal posies can be arranged for a random effect, using four or more different kinds of flower. Take one each of the flowers chosen and form into a small bunch. Bind them together with silver reel or fuse wire. With the bunch in one hand, add another single flower, positioning it at an angle from the main bunch, and bind in (1).

Continue to add all the flowers and foliage, one piece at a time, turning the posy slightly as each new item is bound in. When all the material has been used, wind florist's tape neatly round the stems, bend them slightly to form a handle (2), and finish with a bow or trailing ribbons.

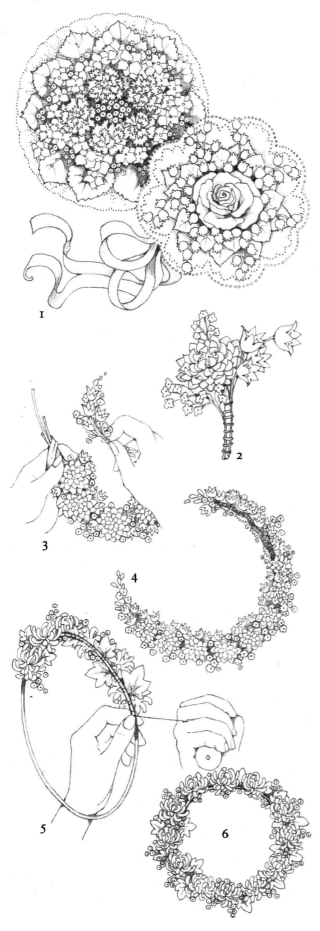

Formal posies

The increasingly popular Victorian posy, with its differently coloured bands of flowers surrounding a central bloom, has a much more formal look than the one described on page 15 and, as its effect depends on the neatness of its construction, will probably need to be wired. Choose a special central bloom and enough flowers of each colour to form three or four circles round it. Shorten the stems of each one and wire them individually as described on page 13; this will enable the central flower to be raised slightly above the rest, and each circle to be level and compact.

Holding the central flower in one hand, place flowers all of the same colour around it. Wind reel or fuse wire lightly round the stems a few times to keep the bunch together while adding the next band of colour. When all the flowers have been bound in, finish with a border frill of lace, or perhaps a circle of evergreen leaves (**1**). Finish as described for informal posies (see figure 2 on page 15).

Head-dresses

Fresh flowers make delightful hair decorations, especially for weddings as garlands in the form of a headband or circlet. The flowers used should match the ones being carried, and appropriate to the wearer: for example, small chrysanthemums and cornflowers would be suitable for a teenage bridesmaid, while a small child should have more delicate flowers such as forget-me-nots and violets.

There are two ways to make a headband forming a half-circle to go at the front or back of the head. One is to take a fine stub wire, covered with tape and cut to the correct length if necessary, and use it as a base on which to bind wired, taped flowers; and the other is to bind the individually wired pieces together without a base wire. In both cases assemble a few sprigs at a time and bind first with reel wire (**2**), then with tape, positioning the flowers so that one side will be flat against the wearer's head. Finish each end with a tapering sprig pointing outwards (**3**), choosing pieces that look similar. Curve the head-dress to the wearer's head (**4**), and secure with hair grips (bobby pins).

A circlet of flowers is made in a similar way, also using wired flowers and leaves. Either use a base of stub wires, twisted together to form a circle which will fit the wearer's head (covered with tape so that it will not scratch), and bind the flowers to it (**5**), or make a 'rope' of flowers by simply binding them together with reel wire and tape and bending the two ends round to form a circle (**6**). Secure the join with more reel wire and cover it with ribbon.

Bouquets

Many otherwise adept flower arrangers consider bouquets difficult to make, but they can be approached simply as flower arrangements to be carried instead of placed in a container.

Unwired bouquets

Presentation bouquets, designed to lie across the arm when carried, should be wired as little as possible since they will probably be stood in water eventually. Informal bridal bouquets like the one pictured on page 14 also require little or no wiring if the flowers lie well together.

To construct an unwired bouquet, simply arrange the flowers in the hand or on a flat surface if you prefer, beginning with strong foliage at the back which will support the flowers, and building up the arrangement from it, with a central focal point and the edges tapering away from this. Bind the flowers together with fine wire (1). When making a trail of flowers to hang down from a bride's bouquet, start with the tip, using small, tapering buds and laying them on a flat surface. Add more material till you have a pleasing shape, bind the stems (2) and position them carefully in the rest of the bouquet. Trim the stems and bind with tape and ribbon.

Wired bouquets

A bouquet in which every flower and leaf has been wired can look natural and still create the desired effect of formality and graceful symmetry. Unlike unwired material, where the natural shape dictates to a large extent the way in which a bouquet is arranged, wired flowers can be arranged at any angle.

Orchids, lilies, chincherinchee, stephanotis, roses and carnations are among the flowers suitable for a wired bouquet. Where only one kind of flower is to predominate, such as roses, include a few sprays of a flower such as lily-of-the-valley for contrast.

Wire each leaf and stem individually as described on page 13; buds and blossoms from the same original stem should also be wired separately. Cover each wired stem with florist's tape, then make sprays by twisting their stems together (3).

To assemble the bouquet according to your design, it is usually easier to make it in two or three sections which are first bound separately and then bound together. For a tapering bouquet, position the smallest flowers for the ends first, building up the bouquet from them (see figure 2). As with any arrangement, put the largest flowers in the centre and smaller ones at the sides. As you reach the top of each section, bend the wires back so that the bouquet flows downwards (4). Bind the stems as above.

Dried & preserved flowers

Dried and preserved flowers can be displayed in all kinds of decorative ways: as they don't need water they can be arranged in wicker baskets, put in lidded jars in layers of different colours, made into heart-shaped keepsakes like the one below (on a florist's foam base), and into festive decorations.

Flowers and herbs can also be dried to preserve their scent. Roses, lavender, mock orange and pinks are just a few of the many flowers that can be used in this way, for pot-pourris and fillings for sachets, sweet bags and pillows, so that the scents of summer can be enjoyed all year round.

With very little equipment you can preserve all kinds of flowers, grasses and leaves. And with a few simple florist's materials, and basic sewing skills for making cushions and sachets, you can easily create all the items described on the following pages.

Some popular plants for preserving

plant name, flower colour	what to dry, when to pick	air drying	powder drying	glycerine*	water drying
Acanthus, bear's breeches; white, lilac	flowers (summer)	●			
Acer pseudoplatanus, sycamore	foliage, fruit (summer, autumn)			●	
Achillea, yarrow; yellow, white	flowers, foliage, seed heads, (summer, autumn)	●			foliage
Allium, ornamental onion; many colours	flowers, seed heads (spring, summer, autumn)	●			
Althaea, hollyhock; many colours	flowers, seed heads (late summer, autumn)	●	●		
Amaranthus caudatus, love-lies-bleeding; crimson, green	flowers (summer)	●			
Anemone, windflower; white, pink, purple, blues, red	flowers (spring, summer, autumn)		●		
Angelica	seed heads (autumn)	●			
Anthriscus sylvestris, cow parsley	seed heads (late summer)	●			
Artemisia absinthium, wormwood; yellow	flowers (summer)	●			
Aucuba, spotted laurel	foliage (early summer)			●	
Azalea; many colours	flowers (late spring)		●		
Briza maxima, quaking grass	seed heads	●			
Calluna, ling; many colours	flowers (late summer)	●			●
Camellia; white, pink, red	flowers, foliage (late spring)		●	●	
Clematis; many colours	flowers, seed heads (spring, summer, autumn)	●	●	seed heads	
Convallaria majalis, lily of the valley	foliage (summer)	● + hot air		●	●
Cortaderia, pampas grass; cream	plumes (late summer)	●			
Cynara scolymus, globe artichoke; purple	flowers (summer)	hot air			
Dahlia; many colours	flowers (summer)		●		
Delphinium, larkspur; blue, purple, white	flowers, seed heads (summer, autumn)	● + hot air	●		flowers
Dianthus, carnation, pink; white, pinks, red, cream	flowers (summer)		●		
Digitalis, foxglove; white, mauve, purple, pink, cream	flowers, seed heads (spring, summer)	seed heads		flowers	
Dipsacus fullonum, teasel	seed heads (late summer)	●		●	
Echinops, globe thistle; blue, white	flowers (summer)	●			
Erica, heather; white, pink, purple	flowers (all year)	●			●
Eryngium, sea holly; blue	flowers (summer)	●		●	
Eucalyptus	foliage			●	
Fagus, beech	foliage			●	
Forsythia; yellow	flowers (spring)		●		
Hedera, ivy	foliage (summer)			●	
Helipterium, rhodanthe; yellow white, pinks	flowers (late summer)	●			
Helleborus, Christmas rose; white, pink, mauve	flowers, foliage (winter)		●	●	

*foliage except where otherwise stated

Plant name, flower colour	what to dry, when to pick	air drying	powder drying	glycerine *	water drying
Helichrysum, everlasting flower; many colours	flowers (summer)	•			
Hyacinth; white, pink, blue	flowers (spring)		•		
Hydrangea; white, pink, blue	flowers (late summer)			flowers	•
Iris (beardless varieties); many colours	seed heads (spring)	•			
Lagurus ovatus, hare's tail grass	seed heads	•			
Lavandula, lavender; mauve, purple, white	flowers (summer)	•			
Laurus nobilis, bay	foliage			•	
Limonium, statice; many colours	flowers (late summer)	•			
Lunaria annua, honesty	seed heads (late summer)	•			
Narcissus, daffodil; yellow, white, cream	flowers (spring)		•		
Papaver orientale, oriental poppy	seed heads (summer)	•			
Paeonia, peony; pinks, reds, white, yellow	flowers, foliage (summer)		•	•	
Physalis franchetii, Chinese lantern	seed heads (summer)	•			
Primula, primrose; yellow, white, pink, red, mauve	flowers (spring)		•		
Quercus, oak	foliage			•	
Rosa, rose; many colours	flowers, foliage (summer)		•	•	
Syringa, lilac; white, mauve	flowers (spring)		•		
Tulipa, tulip; many colours	flowers, seed heads (spring)	seed heads	•		
Viola, pansy, violet; many colours	flowers (spring, summer)		•		

What to preserve

Almost every plant that grows can be preserved in one way or another. Flowers, grasses and foliage can be picked throughout the year, so that a new supply of freshly dried material can always be ready if required.

Flowers The chart of common wild and cultivated flowers on these two pages does not attempt to be comprehensive, so experiment with as many different flowers as you can. Begin with easy plants which dry while still on the plant and only need to be picked at the right moment before they become too brittle: these include Chinese lanterns (*Physalis franchetii*) with their orange bells, and honesty (*Lunaria annua*) with its papery white pods. Equally easy to dry are the so-called everlasting flowers, the most popular of which are the colourful daisy, *Helichrysum*, and the tall statice, *Limonium*, which has small, feathery flowers of many colours.

Many flowers can be preserved by more than one method (see chart); and some species may be dried at different stages of the plant's life, such as *Clematis tangutica* which has yellow bell-shaped flowers followed by silky seed heads, or the ornamental onion (*Allium*), whose globular flower-heads give way to equally decorative seed heads.

Grasses Most grasses dry well and are excellent for tall arrangements. Decorative grasses can be specially grown from seed, the most easily obtainable being quaking grass (*Briza maxima*), hare's tail (*Lagurus ovatus*), fountain grass (*Pennisetum ruppelii*) and feather grass (*Stipa pennata*), but wild grasses found on country walks can also be very decorative.

Foliage Branches of foliage are indispensable for most large arrangements and are not as difficult to preserve as might be thought. Foliage preserved in glycerine (page 25) adds splashes of bold colour to the more subtle tones of many dried-flower arrangements; the leaves do not retain their original colours but turn many shades of cream, brown and red, depending on the species.

When to pick

Flowers and foliage should be in peak condition when picked for drying. If taken too early, the heads and stems of flowers may be too limp to preserve successfully; if picked too late, the flowers may be damaged or beginning to fade or go to seed. Pick plants at midday, after the dew has dried and before there is any chance of frost if it is late in the year. Choose a dry day as plants with even a hint of moisture on them attract mildew.

These arrangements in baskets (left) demonstrate that dried flowers can be as colourful as fresh ones, and that there are many colours to choose from. Use plenty of dried material for a massed, abundant effect and to hide the stalks as much as possible. Since dried flowers and baskets without water are comparatively light, fill the bottom of your container with stones or sand inside a bag to weight it. Next, place florist's foam in the basket, packing it in tightly, and arrange your flowers (wired if necessary – see page 25), studding the foam with them until it is no longer visible. If you want your arrangement to stand on the floor or in a fireplace, work on it at this low level so that you can always assess the final effect of the design. Simple mixed bunches of dried flowers, like the one on the lower left of the picture, look good as wall decorations.

For a taller, domed arrangement, crumple some chicken wire (see page 8) and wedge it into a weighted container to make a mound. Insert stalked flowers into it, or tie flower-heads to the netting with silver reel wire.

This miniature flowering 'tree' (above) has a base of florist's foam covered with wire netting, and a length of branch forming the trunk. To make one similar, take a 45 cm (18 in) length of branch (or use a piece of broom handle), sharpen one end of it and place it, pointed end up, in a 15 cm (6 in) plant pot. Pour plaster of Paris into the pot almost to the brim and, when the plaster is set, push a block of florist's foam about 12 cm (5 in) thick on to the point of the trunk. Bend a piece of chicken wire (see page 8) round the foam to form a globe shape, and fix it to the trunk with a hose clip (see the drawing on page 25).

Insert dried material – air-dried Chinese lanterns, white statice and pine cones are used here – into the foam through the chicken wire, positioning the flowers to keep the shape spherical. Make sure that there are enough flowers low down to cover the retaining clip, and push them firmly into the foam so that they cannot slip out. Put the pot into a wicker basket and cover the plaster of Paris with moss, dried grass or pebbles.

23

Drying and preserving methods

Air drying
This is the simplest and most common way of preserving flowers and grasses. All you need is a cool, dry, airy, preferably dark, place with enough space to hang the drying materials. Strong, rigid stems will not wither after drying, but softer stems may shrivel completely and become too brittle for use in arrangements, and they should be wired (see page 25). Flowers which dry naturally on the plant are best brought inside by early autumn at the latest, before they can be damaged by bad weather. Air drying is not suitable for foliage.

Strip off the leaves and tie up the flowers in small bunches of the same variety. Tie near the end of the stems and ensure that the flower-heads are not bunched together as it is vital for air to circulate around individual blooms. Use thread for delicate stems and string for coarser ones, tying gently but tightly so that the stems will not fall out as they shrink when drying.

Hang the plants upside down, suspended from hooks or a line; a clothes airer on a pulley attached to the ceiling, like the one shown on page 18, is ideal for this, as long as it is in a dry airy place. Drying upside down ensures that the flowers retain their shape and that stems remain straight. Some plants, however, benefit from being dried upright: grasses and tall plants with umbrella-like heads, like cow parsley, may look better with gently curving stems in some arrangements, and if you simply put them in a tall, narrow container, you will find that they naturally adopt slightly curved positions as they dry.

The speed of drying obviously varies from plant to plant, but in general delicate flowers and grasses dry in a week or so, whereas larger plants containing more moisture may need about three weeks. When they are completely dry the plants will feel papery.

Some flowers benefit from being dried quickly in hot air so that they retain their colours. This is the case with many annuals such as clarkia and perennials like delphiniums, and with plants dried for their scents (see page 28). Put them in an airing cupboard, spread out on paper, or on a piece of chicken wire with the heads resting on the wire and the stems hanging below. The flowers should be dry in a few days.

Water drying
Shrubby plants like hydrangeas and those with tough stems such as heathers should be dried with the ends of their stems in water. Do not pick the flower until it is just beginning to dry of its own accord, then stand it in about 12 mm ($\frac{1}{2}$ in) water and leave till this has been absorbed, but do not top up at all.

Powder drying
This method of preservation is ideal for large, single blooms and fragile flower-heads. It relies on the use of desiccants, powdery substances which draw out moisture. Only flowers of the same type should be dried together in this way, as flowers vary in the time they take to dry. Desiccants can all be oven-dried and reused.

Borax and alum are the most popular desiccants. These inexpensive powders, available from chemists, are very light and suit the most delicate flowers. Do not use them for heavier blooms such as chrysanthemums and dahlias, as the fine powders cannot support their weight. Borax and alum act best if mixed together in equal amounts, as borax sticks to the dried flowers if used alone. Plants treated in this way take one to two weeks to lose their moisture and become paper-like.

Silica gel, also available from chemists, is relatively heavy and best suited to strong plants, although the crystals can be crushed to form a finer powder. It is comparatively expensive, but worth using if you wish to dry flowers quickly (in order to keep them as near their original colours as possible), as it works in about four to six days.

Sand is the heaviest desiccant and the slowest to work, taking two weeks or more. Ordinary builder's sand is suitable but must be cleaned before use. Half-fill a bucket with sand, add water and stir. When the sand settles skim off any dirt. Repeat several times, always using clean water, then dry the sand in a low oven and sieve before use. Sand is particularly useful for drying heavy blooms, but if used on more fragile flowers it should be mixed with borax in proportions of one part sand to two parts borax.

To use a desiccant, take an airtight container (such as a cake tin, sandwich box or even a shoe box which can be sealed with adhesive tape) and pour in the powder to a depth of 25 mm (1 in). Gently lay the flower-heads on top of the powder, but not touching. Take a handful of desiccant and trickle it over each bloom (1), making sure that each part of the flower is thoroughly coated. It is a good idea to separate the petals with a light instrument such as a cocktail stick when adding the powder, so that it trickles into all the crevices between them. Pour on more powder to a depth of another 25 mm (1 in), then seal the flowers in the container and put in a warm, dry place.

Preserving with glycerine

Whereas air and powder drying take the moisture from plants, glycerine is used to replace the moisture by being absorbed by the plant, which remains flexible and lifelike. It is most suited to foliage, particularly beech leaves, although a few flowers, such as foxglove, and some seed heads like those of clematis, can also be preserved in this way.

Pick fairly fine branches with established foliage. First clean the leaves, then pare away the bark from the stem ends and split them before plunging them into deep water for a few hours.

Mix one part glycerine with two parts very hot water and stir well. Put the stems into about 10 cm (4 in) of the hot solution and leave in a dark, cool room until all the glycerine has been taken up and the leaves have turned colour. Add more solution if necessary to achieve a uniform shade throughout the plant. Trees with tough leaves – laurel, for example – can take from ten to twelve weeks to absorb the glycerine, whereas those with lighter foliage – such as beech, box and eucalyptus – take only one to three weeks. If glycerine 'beads' gather on the leaves it means they have been in the solution too long. Wipe all leaves and stems with tissues when removing them from the glycerine.

Wiring

Most dried plant stems are too brittle for use in arrangements, and so they must be wired to support the flowers and keep them upright. Ideally, this should be done before drying because pushing wires into papery heads may cause them to fall apart.

You will need: florist's stub wire of appropriate width and length (25 cm (10 in) long and 0.90 mm (20 gauge) is a useful size but there is a wide range from which to choose); and florist's adhesive tape (gutta-percha), available in different colours, for stemless flowers.

Method

To wire stems, carefully push a stub wire up through the centre of the stem as far as possible so that the flower-head cannot flop over (**2**). To wire a head only, cut off the stem so that about 25 mm (1 in) of it remains and insert the wire through this into the base of the flower, taking care that it does not protrude at the top (bend the end if necessary) (**3**). When the flower-head is dry, you can hide the wire by covering it with florist's tape. Now you can arrange the material as required, pushing the stems into a base of florist's foam or chicken wire, or both, as for the 'tree' on page 23 (**4**).

An Advent wreath (above) can be made with a florist's foam ring as a base, or in the same way as a swag or garland, using a base 'rope' (see below). Position the four candles first, using holders to secure them, then decorate round their bases before filling in the gaps between them. You could make an identical wreath (minus candles) to hang on the front door.

A festive swag or garland makes a stunning Christmas decoration, draped round a doorway or window, or hung from a mantlepiece like the one shown here (right). It is made by tying evergreen foliage, dried flowers and seasonal decorations to a base 'rope' of twisted nylons or lengths of cloth, rolled up plastic netting, or even a proper rope about 12 mm ($\frac{1}{2}$ in) in diameter. Arrange the flowers and leaves in bunches and attach them to the base rope by wrapping reel wire or twine tightly round the stalks and then round the rope. Work from the ends inwards, pointing the bunches outwards, and keeping the design symmetrical. Finally, add wired fir cones, berry clusters and ribbons, tying them in where there are gaps, and fix the swag in place with drawing pins, adhesive clay (see page 8) or tape.

Drying scented plants

Many flowers and herbs with distinctive scents can be dried for use in fragrant pot-pourris, sachets and pillows. Suggestions for suitable plants for different uses are given below, but do experiment with different combinations. In general all scented material for drying should be picked in its prime (see page 21). Herbs should be taken just before they flower. Pick them with long stems to avoid bruising the petals and leaves.

As scent and colour tend to be lost by cool air drying it is better to strip petals and leaves for perfumery from their stalks, scatter them over a tray, and dry them in hot air (see page 24).

Pot-pourris

Used to scent the air, these are made up primarily of dried, scented flowers and herbs mixed with oils and spices, and presented in attractive containers. Among the many flowers suitable for use in pot-pourris are carnations and pinks, heliotrope, honeysuckle, hyacinths, jasmine, lavender, lily-of-the-valley, marigolds, mock orange, narcissus, pansies, roses and violets. Suitable herbs include angelica, basil, bay, bergamot, borage, lemon balm, marjoram, mints, rosemary, sage, sweet Cicely, tarragon, thyme and verbena.

To retard the evaporation of their scents, the dried plants need a fixative. The most usual fixative is dried, ground orris root, but the ground roots of angelica and sweet Cicely can also be used, as can gum benzoin, available in powder form. The peel from lemons or oranges, dried slowly on a wire tray in hot air and then crushed to a fine powder, also makes a good fixative. Common salt is used in moist pot-pourris.

Oils and spices are also needed to enhance the fragrance of pot-pourris. Commonly used oils include lavender, rose and jasmine as individual fragrances, and you can also buy blended pot-pourri oils. Crushed spices such as allspice, cinnamon, cloves, coriander and nutmeg add more piquant aromas. They can be mixed in advance then stored till needed, say in the proportions of one tablespoon of each of the spices to two tablespoons of fixative.

Dry pot-pourri

The following recipe is a quick and easy way of making a strongly scented dry pot-pourri.

You will need: equal quantities of dried roses, lavender, carnations, lemon balm or verbena, scented pelargonium leaves, honeysuckle, pansies, marjoram and rosemary to make up 9 litres (2 gal); 30 g (1 oz) each of crushed orris root and gum benzoin; 15 g ($\frac{1}{2}$ oz) each crushed cloves, cinnamon and nutmeg; and a few drops each of rose, citrus and jasmine oil (or a blended oil).

Method

Put the dried flowers and herbs into a bowl and add the fixative, then the oils and spices. Stir and arrange in pretty containers, with whole brightly coloured flowers on top for decoration. Dry pot-pourris such as this lose their scent after a time, so the mixture should be refreshed occasionally by adding, say, a piece of dried citrus peel, a pinch of spice and a drop of scented oil.

Moist pot-pourri

Moist pot-pourris, or sweet jars, retain their scent much longer than the dry versions, but take longer to mature. The following recipe is for a basic mixed moist pot-pourri.

You will need: equal quantities of partly dried carnations, lily-of-the-valley, mock orange, roses and violets to make up 9 litres (2 gal); 115 g (4 oz) salt; 90 g (3 oz) orris root powder; a few drops of mixed flower oil; and a tablespoon each of crushed cinnamon, cloves and nutmeg.

Method

Add the orris root powder, oil and spices to the flowers and mix well. Put a 5 cm (2 in) layer of flowers in a wide jar and sprinkle over a thin layer of salt. Repeat these layers until the jar is full. Seal the jar and leave it for at least a month, shaking or stirring frequently, then put into small china jars.

Scented bags

To make a bag to hold a pot-pourri or herb mixture for a linen sachet or inner pillow bag, use a natural fine fabric such as muslin, lawn or voile, to allow the scent to come through. The most familiar scented bag is one filled with lavender but you could use a mixture of, say, half lavender and half lemon balm, or lavender and rose petals plus lemon verbena. Spices can also be added, and so can a fixative if necessary.

Cut out two pieces of the fabric to the required size, sew double seams round three sides and turn it inside out. Fill the bag with the mixture and sew up the fourth side. For a pillow or cushion, wrap a double thickness of quilting wadding round the bag, to form a cushion pad – there is no need to sew down the edges of the wadding – and insert it into a cushion cover so that it fits tightly (see pages 32–3 for some ideas for covers).

Lavender bag

The following instructions are for a lavender bag 15 cm (6 in) square (photograph on page 30). Its lattice of white ribbon contrasts attractively with the mauve voile of the inner bag visible behind it.

You will need: 80 cm (32 in) broderie anglaise ribbon 45 mm (1¾ in) wide; 80 cm (32 in) white satin ribbon 6 mm (¼ in) wide; 1 m (40 in) mauve satin ribbon 12 mm (½ in) wide; mauve voile 40 cm (16 in) square; white lawn 20 cm (8 in) square; white cotton thread; 60 g (2 oz) dried lavender.

Method
Cut the broderie anglaise ribbon into four 20 cm (8 in) lengths. With right sides and scalloped edges of two lengths together, sew a diagonal seam from one corner by the raw edge at a 45° angle down to the scalloped edge (**1**). Pull the two lengths of ribbon apart and you will see that a 90° angle, the first corner of the bag front, has been made.

Join all the lengths of ribbon to each other in this way, to form a broderie anglaise 'frame' (**2**). Trim the seams and press flat.

Place the frame wrong side up. Cut lengths of white satin ribbon to form a criss-cross pattern over the area within the frame, and tack in position. With the frame right side up, sew all round it, close to the curves of the scalloped edge, to secure the ends of the satin ribbon (**3**).

Fold the mauve ribbon in half lengthways and sew the edges together to form a thin strip. Pin the ribbon, edges outwards, round the right side of the frame, 12 mm (½ in) from the edge, starting at one corner, and sew in place. When you come to the final open corner, finish off by turning the ends of the ribbon back in on themselves to form neat edges (**4**), then sew the two ends together at the back, using small hand stitches.

Right sides together, pin the white lawn for the backing to the broderie anglaise and sew round three sides. Turn right side out.

Cut two pieces of voile 6 mm (¼ in) smaller all round than the outer cover, make it into a scented bag (see page 28) and fill with just enough lavender to plump it out. Machine the open end of the bag closed, then insert it into the outer cover (**5**) and hand sew the last seam closed.

If you wish to hang the bag, use the remainder of the mauve ribbon to make decorative loops, as shown (**6**), and sew them on to one corner of the bag.

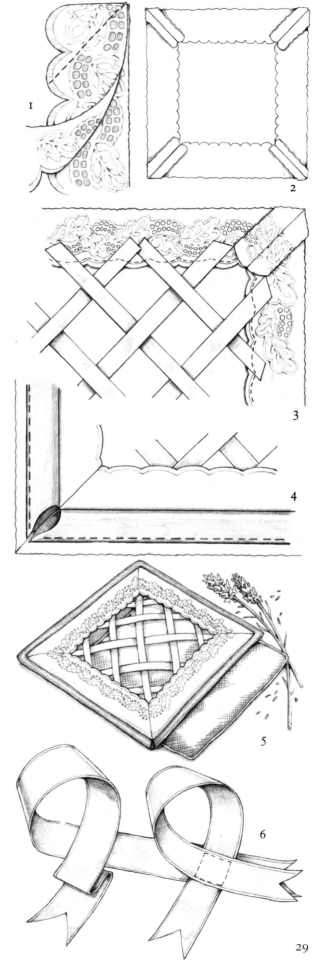

A bowl of pot-pourri (right) will give the air of a room a delightful fragrance. Many of the flowers used to make them – even most pot-pourri mixtures themselves – can also be used to fill sachets and sweet bags for scenting clothes and linen. You could even make a scented pincushion. There are almost as many recipes for pot-pourri as there are flowers, and in time you will have the confidence to create your own favourite perfumes; instructions for two basic pot-pourris are on page 28. To make the lavender bag and scented pincushion (above) see pages 29 and 32 respectively.

Pillows and cushions with a scented bag inside them (right) can be used in bed to promote sleep or relieve a headache, or simply scattered about a room to create an atmosphere of freshness. Fillings could be dried hops on their own (thought to be best for insomniacs) or mixtures using, say, angelica, borage, chamomile, dill, elder flowers and lavender, all of which make sweet-scented pillows. To make a scented bag see page 28; to make the cushion covers see pages 32–3.

Scented pincushion

The following instructions are for attaching a scented pincushion to the lid of a round raffia work-basket about 14 cm (5½ in) in diameter (photograph on page 30).

You will need: 20 cm (8 in) quilting wadding; 20 cm (8 in) muslin; flowered cotton fabric about 20 cm (8 in) square to cover the top; 60 g (2 oz) dried lavender or pot-pourri; tacking thread; 50 cm (20 in) decorative braid or ribbon; matching thread.

Method

Cut out two circles of wadding, one the same size as the lid, the other 10 mm (⅜ in) smaller all round. Cut two muslin circles the same size as the smaller wadding circle. Sew the two muslin circles together round their edges with two rows of stitches about 3 mm (⅛ in) apart, leaving a small gap between the two ends of the stitching.

Using a small funnel or rolled up piece of paper, pour the lavender or pot-pourri mixture into the muslin pouch through the opening (**1**) until it is packed full. Sew up the opening and tack the pouch to the small circle of wadding, round the edges, then pin and tack the large circle of wadding to the other side of the pouch, so that the pouch is totally enclosed.

Cut a circle of flowered fabric 14 cm (5½ in) in diameter and place it on top of the larger wadding circle, easing the fabric over it, and tack in place. Use a zigzag stitch to sew the fabric to the pouch round the edges, machining through all the layers.

Pin the pouch in place on the lid and, with a strong needle and double cotton, sew it down (**2**), making sure that the stitches go through all the layers of the pouch and the lid. Finally, finish off by sewing a length of decorative ribbon or braid round the pincushion, over the raw edges of the fabric.

Patchwork cushion cover

Simple diamond shapes and one central hexagon make up this patchwork flower motif (shown on page 31). To save time you can buy ready-made templates from craft and needlework shops. The cover is for a scented cushion 35 cm (14 in) square.

You will need: green cotton fabric 80 cm × 100 cm (32 in × 40 in); two pieces of 30 cm × 100 cm (12 in × 40 in) cotton fabric, one plain pink, one patterned; a 30 cm (12 in) toning zip; matching thread; 150 cm (59 in) narrow piping cord (gauge 2); 50 paper diamonds and 1 paper hexagon, cut from templates; bias fabric strip to match petals.

Method

Use the paper shapes to cut out one patterned hexagon, six pink and twelve patterned diamonds for the petals, and thirty-two green diamonds for the background (all with seam allowance). Join the pink diamonds to each other by putting two patches together, right sides facing, and oversewing. Sew the patterned 'petals' to the pink ones and finally add the outer layer of green diamonds in the pattern shown (**1**). Remove the paper shapes and iron the seams.

Cut out a cushion back from the rest of the green cotton, adding a 12 mm (½ in) seam allowance all round. Position this on the patchwork centrally and draw round it with a ruler and chalk. Trim patchwork to the size of the backing (**2**).

Centre the piping cord along the wrong side of the bias fabric strip, then turn the fabric over the cord and pin. Sew the length of the fabric close to the cord, to hold it in place, but leave the ends unsewn (**3**). Pin the piping all round the right side of the patchwork front, making sure that it is lying on the seam line 12 mm (½ in) from the edge. The raw edges of the piping fabric and the raw edges of the patchwork should be parallel. Sew in position except at the ends of the bias fabric. Seam these two ends together where they meet, bind the two ends of cord together with thread (**4**) and finish sewing the binding to the cover.

To insert the zip, place one edge of the opened zip along one edge of the patchwork, right sides together, so that the zipper teeth are lying along the piping. Pin, tack and sew in place (**5**), keeping as close to the zip teeth and piping as you can (use a zipper or a piping foot). In the same way, sew the other half of the zip to the cushion back. Sew the patchwork front to the cushion back along the other three sides. Finish off the zip ends and any raw edges, and turn right side out.

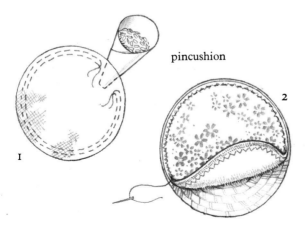

pincushion

Lace cushion cover

This cushion cover (illustrated on page 31) is for a scented cushion 40 cm (16 in) square (see page 28).

You will need: floral curtain lace 50 cm × 120 cm (20 in × 48 in); fine, pale blue voile 50 cm × 120 cm (20 in × 48 in); a 35 cm (14 in) zip to match lace; 180 cm (72 in) cotton lace trim; matching thread.

Method
Cut the curtain lace into two equal pieces, allowing for 12 mm (½ in) seams all round. Cut two pieces of voile the same size. Tack one of the voile pieces to the wrong side of each piece of lace. Position the cotton lace trim, facing inwards, along the edges of the right side of one of the lace and voile rectangles, and sew in place (**6**).

Insert the zip fastener, following the method given for the patchwork cushion (figure 5), but treating the lace as the piping. Sew the two layers of the front to the two layers of the back, right sides together, along the remaining three sides. Trim the corners, then finish off the zip ends. Turn the cover right side out and sew up the ends of the lace.

Broderie anglaise cushion cover

This cushion cover (illustrated on page 31) is for a scented cushion pad 40 cm × 25 cm (16 in × 10 in) (see page 28).

You will need: broderie anglaise, with a regular pattern through which ribbon can be threaded, 30 cm × 100 cm (12 in × 36 in); 140 cm (55 in) broderie anglaise ribbon trimming; a 35 cm (14 in) matching zip; nine 50 cm (20 in) lengths of 6 mm (¼ in) satin ribbon in different pastel colours (here green, yellow, pink, blue and mauve); thread.

Method
Cut the broderie anglaise into two oblong pieces, allowing for a 12 mm (½ in) seam round all sides. Following the instructions for the lace cushion, sew on the broderie anglaise trim, insert the zip, then make up the cover.

Now thread the satin ribbon in and out of the eyelets in the broderie anglaise with a large needle, to make nine rows, leaving about 5 cm (2 in) of ribbon at either end of each row. Loop these ends back on to the cover, and sew them in position with a row of stitching along the edge of the cover where the broderie anglaise trim is inserted (**7**).

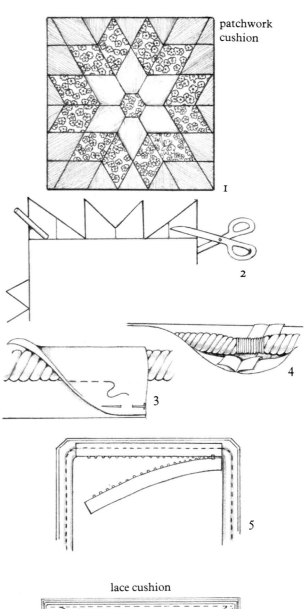

patchwork cushion

lace cushion

broderie anglaise cushion

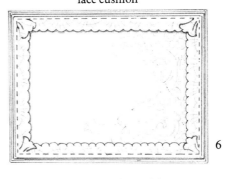

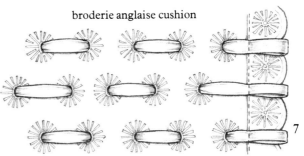

Pressed flowers

Using pressed flowers is one of the simplest and most satisfying crafts. Patience, neat-handedness and a love of flowers are all you need to create your own floral pictures and original gifts. Many wild and cultivated flowers picked on summer days can easily be turned into decorative and useful items like the table mat, greetings cards and gift tag pictured on these two pages.

Flowers and leaves only need a few weeks under a weight, whether it is a pile of heavy books or a proper botanical press, in order to be ready for use. In nearly all the projects described in this chapter the pressed plants are simply glued to a paper background, then protected under glass or plastic. No special equipment is required, although a flower press would be worth making or buying if you decide to turn this into a regular hobby, since it is the neatest and most efficient way of pressing flowers.

35

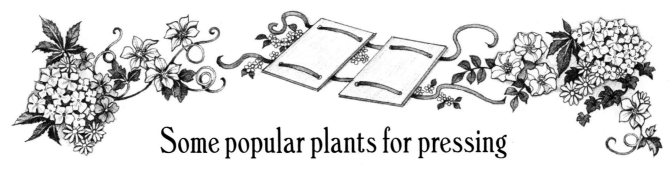

Some popular plants for pressing

plant name, flower colour	what & when to pick	colour after pressing
Acer, maple species	foliage (autumn)	red, brown, yellow, etc.
Anthemis, chamomile; white	flowers, stalks (summer)	white
Anthriscus sylvestris, cow parsley; white	flowers (summer)	white
Bellis perennis, lawn daisy; white	flowers, stalks (spring, summer)	white
Calendula officinalis, pot marigold; orange-yellow	flowers (summer)	orange-yellow
Caltha palustris, marsh marigold; yellow	whole (summer)	yellow then beige
Campanula rotundifolia, harebell; pale blue	flowers, foliage (summer)	pure white
Clematis; many colours	flowers, foliage and stalks (summer)	mauve shades turn brown
Convallaria majalis, lily-of-the-valley; white	flowers (summer)	white
Crocosmia × *crocosmiiflora*, montbretia; lemon-yellow to deep orange	flowers, foliage (summer)	remains the same
Cytisus, broom; cream to yellow	flowers (spring and summer)	remains the same
Delphinium, larkspur; many colours	flowers (summer)	blues remain true
Endymion nonscriptus, bluebell; blue-purple	flowers (spring)	pale blue to cream
Fraxinus, ash	foliage (spring)	black
Galanthus, snowdrop; white	flowers (early spring)	white
Geranium species, cranesbill; blue, purple, pink	flowers, foliage (summer)	remains the same
Hedera, ivy	leaves (summer)	brown, black
Hydrangea; white, pink, blue	flowers (summer)	remains the same
Jasminum nudiflorum, winter-flowering jasmine; bright yellow	flowers (winter)	soft yellow to beige
Laburnum; yellow	flowers (late spring)	yellow
Lobelia; blue, white	flowers (summer)	blues remain true
Lunaria annua, honesty; purple, purple and white	flowers, seed pod (summer, autumn)	pod turns silvery
Moluccella laevis, bells of Ireland, white	flowers (summer)	white
Myosotis, forget-me-not; blue, pink, white	flowers, foliage (spring)	remains the same
Narcissus, daffodil; yellow, white, cream	flowers (spring)	remains the same
Nigella, love-in-a-mist; blue, pink	flowers, foliage (summer)	blues fade quickly
Paeonia, peony; many colours	flowers, foliage (summer)	pinks and reds turn wine to dark brown
Papaver species, poppy; many colours	flowers (summer)	orange-reds turn pink
Parthenocissus, Virginia creeper	foliage (autumn)	reds remain
Pelargonium species; red, pink, white	flowers, foliage (summer, autumn)	remains the same
Primula vulgaris, primrose; creamy-yellow	flowers, stalks (spring)	white, pale yellow to yellowy-green
Ranunculus, buttercup, celandine; yellow	flowers, stalks (summer)	turns white in time
Rosa, rose; many colours	flowers (summer)	reds turn brown, many others become cream
Sambucus, elder; creamy-white	flowers (summer)	beige
Solidago, golden rod; yellow	flowers (summer)	yellow
Thymus serpyllum, thyme; purple, pink	flowers (summer)	remains the same
Trifolium, clover; pink, white	whole (summer)	remains the same
Vicia, vetch; mauve	flowers, foliage (summer)	mauve
Viola, pansy, violet; many colours	flowers, stalks (spring, summer)	violet turns brown, other shades darken

What to press

The best flowers for pressing are generally fairly small, fine and flat; they include daisies, primroses, violets and buttercups. Larger, multiple blooms like lupins, hydrangeas and foxgloves rarely press satisfactorily as a whole but they can be broken up into individual florets and pressed separately; you can then reassemble them or, for a more delicate effect, use them singly. Bulky or succulent flowers such as freesias and daffodils are also difficult to press unless you slice the flowers cleanly in half lengthways, with a craft knife or razor blade (1–3), and press and use the halves as separate flowers. Don't use flowers with hard, fleshy centres or very many large petals – pompon dahlias and chrysanthemums, for example – unless you strip off their petals and press them singly for use in made-up blooms.

Not only flower-heads but also some stems and leaves (see chart) can be pressed successfully, as long as they are not thick, hard or brittle. Even some types of fine or feathery seaweed make good pressed material: prepare it by first immersing it in water so that it reverts to its natural shape, then sliding a piece of paper beneath it and lifting it out of the water. Allow the excess water to drain away before placing the still-damp seaweed between blotting paper and pressing as described on page 40. Grasses and ferns also press well if they are not bulky but fairly flat and delicate in structure.

In some cases a pressed flower-head no longer looks at home with its own stalk and foliage but relates much better to those from other blooms. Daisy leaves, for instance, do not press well and lose their colour, but a small *Senecio* leaf, which looks very similar, will help recreate a most realistic lawn daisy. By contrast, the soft stems of the daisy press easily and can be used with many other flower-heads whose own stems are unsuitable for pressing.

Colour changes Most plant material does not retain its original colour when pressed and slowly fades with time. However, much fading and discolouration is caused by the retention of moisture when the flowers are being pressed, and this can largely be avoided if they are dried as much as possible straight after being picked (see page 40). The chart on the facing page shows the colour changes to be expected after pressing some of the most suitable plants.

As a rule, yellow and orange flowers such as buttercups and celandines retain their colours, whereas blue and red flowers fade or turn beige or brown. Young green foliage does not press very well, changing to dirty yellow, grey or even black, but the rich colours of autumn leaves from the various maples, crab-apples and Virginia creeper are retained after pressing, and look very attractive in pressed flower pictures. Variegated ivy leaves turn brown or black, but still lend interest to many designs.

When and how to pick

Pick plants for pressing when they are at their best (generally in spring and summer), on dry days during the middle of the morning or afternoon. Flowers picked at noon on a hot day tend to disintegrate when pressed, while those picked early or late in the day may well be covered with dew and will go mouldy in the press. If you must pick after rain, gently wipe off excess moisture with a tissue and leave the flowers on blotting paper for an hour or so before pressing. Plants which are going to seed should not be pressed, although dried seed heads such as honesty can, of course, be used to add texture to a pressed flower project.

To avoid damaging garden flowers as you pick them, put them side by side in a large basket – a trug is ideal – so that they do not become squashed or bruised. Wild flowers should be transported either in large polythene bags (a few specimens per bag) secured with a rubber band, or on a layer of damp cotton wool in a plastic sandwich box.

Remove the flowers from their temporary homes as soon as you can, and if they have wilted do not put them in water, but press them straight away.

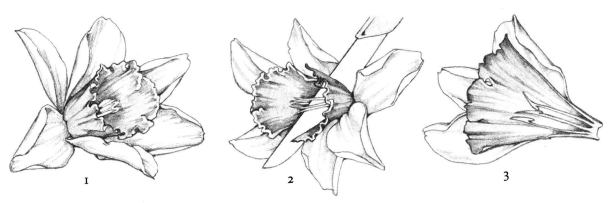

1   2   3

One of the most permanent ways of using pressed flowers is to make them into pictures (left). All you need is a suitable glazed frame with backing board and hanging fixtures, a piece of good-quality stiff paper or card to fit, on which to mount the flowers, a latex adhesive such as Copydex, scissors, a fine paintbrush and blunt-ended tweezers.

Begin with simple arrangements such as one large flower-head surrounded by a few smaller ones, or a small spring-like bouquet, and take time to position the plants until you have achieved a pleasing result. Handle the material as little as possible, using a paintbrush or tweezers to position it. (See also the instructions for cards and gift tags, page 44.) Before gluing the plants in place with spots of adhesive, position the frame over the card to ensure that you have left a good margin round the flowers. As you gain confidence you will be able to go on to more complex arrangements, perhaps mounting the plants on a fabric background such as silk.

Similar methods are employed for another good way of preserving pressed flowers permanently, which is to use them to decorate the covers of books. Photograph albums, address books, scrap books and diaries like the one shown here (above) are all most suitable. You can stick the flowers directly to the cover of the book (if it is smooth in texture and a suitable colour), adding other touches such as strips of ribbon to the corners, or else apply them to a piece of strong decorative paper or plain fabric cut to the size of the book, plus 75 mm (3 in) all round, for folding. The book jacket can then be folded round the book and glued lightly in place, then covered with a sheet of clear self-adhesive film such as Transpaseal, cut slightly larger all round than the paper or fabric; this will protect the flowers from damage when the book is handled. For more detailed information on using flowers and applying Transpaseal, see the instructions for cards and gift tags on page 44.

Pressing flowers

Once you have gathered your flowers, leaves and stalks and ensured that they are dry to the touch, it is best to press them immediately. If you intend to press flowers regularly, then it is worth buying or making a special press (see page 41), but satisfactory results can be achieved by using a heavy book and putting the plant material between its pages. Do not press flowers in a book that you do not want to spoil, but keep an old one just for the purpose.

If you are away from home and don't have the right equipment with you, it is possible to press a few flowers (between sheets of newspaper, paper handkerchiefs or toilet tissue) inside a magazine or paperback, as long as you transfer them to something more appropriate as soon as you can. With these improvised methods of flower pressing, always put an even, heavy weight on top of the flowers, such as more books or telephone directories.

You will need: blotting paper, tissues or other absorbent paper; cardboard or corrugated paper; a flower press or equivalent (see above); a small paintbrush or blunt-ended tweezers for arranging flowers in the press; scissors, a sharp craft knife or razor blade for dissecting 'difficult' plants; adhesive tape to secure stalks if necessary.

Method
Arrange plants for pressing in groups – thick, thin, foliage, grasses, and so on – to ensure that similar types and thicknesses of plants receive the same pressure and will therefore be dry at the same time, and will also be available together for easy reference when you come to use them. Make sure that you press enough flowers at one time for a particular

I

project (for small cards and gift tags you will not need many), and always label them with their names and the date of pressing.

Cut away very thick stems and press down any awkwardly shaped leaves or centres with thumb and fingers. In general, though, the flowers should be handled as little as possible; a fine paintbrush and a pair of blunt-ended tweezers are useful tools for positioning delicate petals and stems. Small pieces of adhesive tape can be used to secure unruly stalks or those you wish to curve into an attractive shape (1). Put as many flowers as can be accommodated on one sheet of blotting paper without them touching. If the petals of a flower overlap each other, separate them with small pieces of tissue paper.

All but the finest, most delicate material will probably retain enough moisture in its tissues to encourage the growth of mould which will cause the subsequent deterioration and fading of the flowers. To prevent this, prepare the material as usual and put it in the press, but look at it again after a day or two. If the blotting paper is at all damp, change it for dry paper (the old blotting paper may be reused as soon as it has dried). Repeat this procedure after a few more days, and again if necessary, until the paper remains dry. Do not add any more fresh plants to the press as these may make the partly dried ones damp again. As soon as the flowers are dry you can tighten the wing nuts on the press to exert greater pressure.

Total pressing time obviously depends on the type of plant and its moisture content, but generally all flowers should be kept in the press for at least six weeks. However, the longer you can wait the better, since some flowers can take up to a year to fade completely. This is particularly important if you are making a flower picture (see pages 38–9), where the ultimate colour of a flower (and therefore its permanence) is more important than on, say, a greetings card.

There are several ways of hastening the pressing process, which, though not as satisfactory as the slow method, can be used if you need some pressed flowers in a hurry. One of these is to keep the press in a warm, dry atmosphere such as a small, sunny, centrally heated room or an airing cupboard for a few days. The resulting flowers will look pressed but will need even more careful handling than usual as this method tends to make them rather brittle. A still faster way of pressing plant material is to use an iron. Put the plants between two sheets of blotting paper and press them with a medium iron for a few minutes, then put them in an airing cupboard, still in the blotting paper and with heavy weights on top, for at least twenty-four hours. Leaves are most suitable for this method.

To make a press

A simple, convenient, lightweight press can easily be made from two sheets of strong cardboard, with a hole punched at each corner and two lengths of ribbon inserted through the holes (1). Put the flowers between sheets of blotting paper or newspaper (preferably both), fold over the top sheet of cardboard and tie the ribbons tightly (2). This quickly made press is ideal for taking on holiday.

If you intend to press flowers often, it is worth using a special botanical press. Various good commercial presses are available, the most popular being made of two squares of plywood held together at each corner with a bolt and wing nut with which the pressure on the flowers can be adjusted. The following instructions are for a press of this design which is simple to make and much cheaper than a bought one.

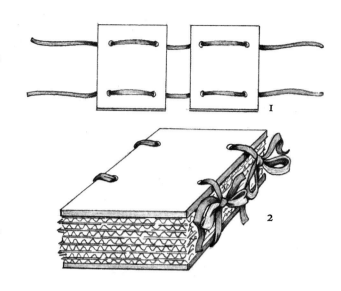

You will need: two pieces of wood at least 30 cm (12 in) square and 20 mm ($\frac{3}{4}$ in) thick (obviously, the larger the press the more flowers can be dried at once); four bolts about 10 cm (4 in) long and 1 cm ($\frac{3}{8}$ in) in diameter, with washers and wing nuts; a drill with a 1 cm ($\frac{3}{8}$ in) bit; several sheets of plywood or corrugated paper, and blotting paper, all cut to fit between the bolts of the press.

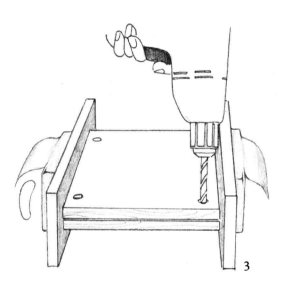

Method

Drill a hole through each corner of the two pieces of wood, holding them together in a clamp to ensure that the holes match (3). The press is now ready for use. Prepare flowers for pressing by putting them between sheets of blotting paper as already described. Put each 'sandwich' of flowers and paper between layers of corrugated paper or plywood, place them all in the press (4), insert the four bolts and tighten the wing nuts (5).

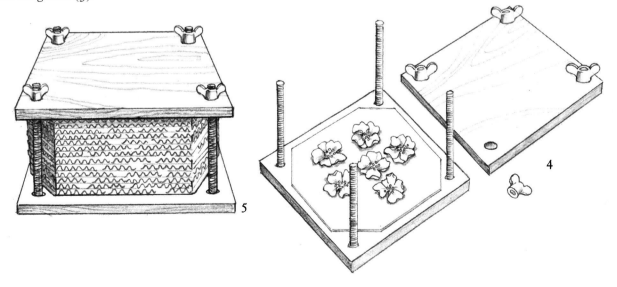

To create unusual candles like these (above), all you need are some white candles, a selection of pressed flowers, leaves and stalks, two or three metal spoons and some translucent paraffin wax. Heat the spoons by plunging them in very hot water, then quickly dry each one before use. Position a flower on the candle, holding it in place with the fingers, and use the back of a hot spoon to press the flower into the wax, which will be slightly soft. Add more flowers in this way until the design is complete, always using a heated spoon and blowing on the flowers to cool them.

In a saucepan, gently and slowly heat enough paraffin wax to cover the candles when they are held upright. Test the wax with a thermometer until it reaches 99°C (210°F) then, holding each candle by the wick, dip it into the molten wax for a few seconds, then hold it in the air for about half a minute until the wax hardens. The candle will look cloudy at first but the surface will clear as the wax cools.

To make the book mark and paperweight shown here (right), see the instructions on page 45. To decorate a mount for a picture, cut the mounting card to size and attach the flowers in the same way as for cards and gift tags (see page 44).

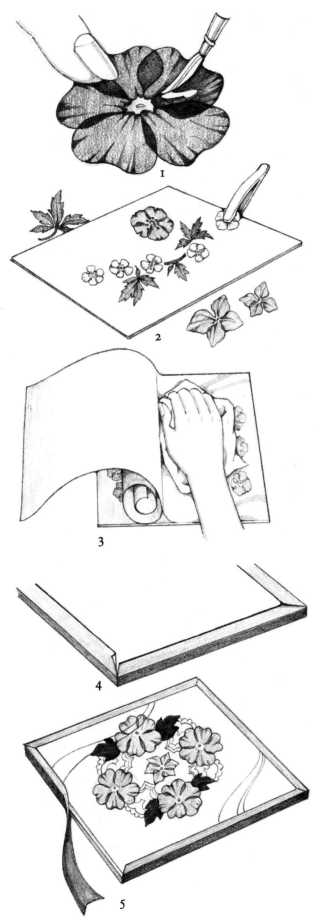

Cards & gift tags

Beautiful hand-made greetings cards and gift tags (like the ones shown on pages 34–5) are easy to make and certain to be kept long after ordinary bought cards have been thrown away. Lace, ribbon, paper doilies and even pictures cut from other cards or magazines can all be used as decorations with pressed flowers.

You will need: pressed flowers; lace, doilies, or other decorations (optional); stiff paper or thin card cut to the appropriate sizes; latex adhesive such as Copydex; clear self-adhesive plastic film such as Transpaseal (optional); fine paintbrush; blunt-ended tweezers; scissors; a hole punch and ribbon for gift tags.

Method

First arrange your pressed flowers on the paper, without gluing them, until you have formed a pleasing arrangement. Handle them carefully, with the aid of a paintbrush and tweezers (1 and 2). To fix the plants in position, apply glue sparingly to the underside of each flower, leaf or stalk, again using brush and tweezers to manipulate the plants. Use lace or doilies in the design if you wish, or glue a picture inside the card and make a 'frame' for it by cutting an oval from the front of the card and putting pressed flowers round it.

To protect the design you can cover it with self-adhesive transparent film, although this is not absolutely essential with ephemeral items such as cards. The film requires careful handling, and it is a good idea to practise using it on scraps of paper first, as it creases easily and can form unsightly air bubbles. Start by peeling away the backing from one edge of the film, then place this edge in position on the card, leaving a margin for folding if you wish. Gradually peel away more of the backing, smoothing the film with a paper tissue as you do so (3).

When all the backing has been removed, any margins can be pressed round the edges of the card or tag. To finish a tag, punch a hole in one corner and thread a length of ribbon through it for attaching it to a gift.

Table mats

Pressed flowers can be preserved in a useful as well as pretty way in table mats (see photograph on page 34). A simple way of making them is to use a picture-framing kit of a suitable size, and back it with felt.

You will need: pressed flowers; glass or perspex and stiff card or hardboard cut to the dimensions required, say 25 × 20 cm (10 × 8 in) (or a picture framing kit), coloured paper and a piece of felt or other woollen fabric, all cut to the same measurements as the glass and hardboard; fabric tape of a suitable colour (the type used for joining carpets, with an adhesive backing, is ideal); a paper doily to fit the mat (optional); latex adhesive such as Copydex; scissors, paintbrush and tweezers.

Method
Stick the coloured paper to one side of the card or hardboard. Position the flowers on the paper, using a doily for a background if you wish, making sure that the margins are kept clear. Glue the arrangement in position, then put the glass or perspex on top and bind the edges with fabric tape in a colour that complements the flowers, mitring the corners (4 and 5). Finally, stick on the felt backing.

Paperweight

A floral paperweight (see photograph on page 43) makes an original and very pretty gift, and is extremely simple to make, using a ready-made glass paperweight with a slightly recessed base. These are available from craft shops. A single, flawless flower which fits the recess snugly looks particularly effective preserved in this way, but you could use several smaller ones instead.

You will need: a glass paperweight with recessed base; pressed flower(s); clear matt lacquer or Barbola varnish (from artist's suppliers); a fine paintbrush; a piece of white or cream satin and a piece of felt or other soft fabric slightly smaller than the diameter of the paperweight (optional); clear general-purpose adhesive such as Uhu.

Method
Turn the paperweight upside down and drop a few drops of lacquer or varnish on to the recess with a fine brush (6), then tip the paperweight from side to side to spread the varnish over the surface (7). Place the flower gently in position on this wet surface, then add another thin layer of varnish, again in drops and spreading it by tipping the paperweight. This glues the flower in place and protects it from the air. Continue building up thin layers in this way, allowing two or three days for each one to dry, until the varnish is flush with the rim of the paperweight. Now apply a line of adhesive to the rim of the paperweight and stick the piece of satin centrally over the base, right side towards the flower. Finally, glue the felt to the satin.

Book mark

The charming book mark shown on page 43 is based on a length of satin ribbon, which is decorated with pressed flowers and two more narrow strips of ribbon, then backed with thin card. It is covered on both sides with a protective layer of clear plastic film. Choose the colours of the ribbon to complement the colours of the flowers.

You will need: a length of 4 cm (1½ in) wide satin ribbon (the book mark shown measures 29 cm (11½ in) long); a length of 25 mm (1 in) wide satin ribbon in a toning colour (18 cm (7 in) long for the book mark shown); pressed flowers; thin card cut to same size as the wide ribbon; latex adhesive such as Copydex; clear self-adhesive plastic film such as Transpaseal; paintbrush, tweezers, scissors.

Method
Using a paintbrush and tweezers, arrange the pressed flowers on the wide ribbon (see also the instructions for cards on page 44), cutting lengths of narrow ribbon to fit round them to form a pleasing pattern. Cut the ends of the ribbon into points, and glue them and the flowers in position. Dab spots of glue on one side of the card and stick the decorated ribbon on it. Finally, cover both sides of the book mark with clear plastic film (see the instructions for cards on page 44) and cut one end into a point, through all the layers. The film will prevent the ends of the ribbon from fraying.

paperweight

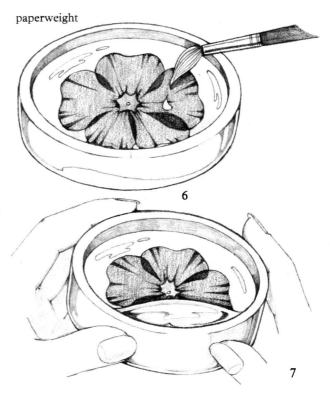

6

7

Stencilled flowers

The craft of stencilling – applying colour or metallic powder to a surface through cutout sections of a piece of paper – originated in China thousands of years ago, was raised to an art form by the Japanese who specialized in stencilling on fabric, and became popular with early American settlers and the Victorians.

With simple stencils and different kinds of paint you too can create stunning effects which will transform all sorts of items, ranging from clothing to blinds to storage jars, or even, as here, a piece of furniture. On the following pages the techniques for stencilling on walls, floors, fabrics, glass, paper, wood and metal are described in detail, so that you will be able to decorate all kinds of surfaces and plan coordinated designs for a room by, say, repeating the same wall frieze pattern on curtains and cushions.

Until quite recently the most usual way to paint a stencil was to use a blunt-ended brush called a stipple brush and a dryish paint, but using spray paint is becoming a more and more popular way of creating stencil designs. With all types of paint for stencilling, it is most important that you practise using it before starting to stencil, so that you know how it will behave on your chosen surface.

Tools & materials

Stencils Ready-made stencils can be bought from crafts shops and art suppliers, singly or in kits containing several stencils which can be combined in different ways to make a variety of patterns and borders. Stencils are made from non-porous material such as specially treated paper or thin sheets of acetate or plastic, so that they can be used many times without becoming soaked with paint. Unless the surface you wish to decorate is absolutely flat, paper-based stencils are easiest to use. Stencil paper is also available so that you can make your own stencils.

Paint *Cellulose spray paint*, used for touching up car bodywork, is available in aerosol cans in a very wide range of attractive colours and is an effective and simple way of creating stencil designs on all kinds of surfaces, including fabric. It is extremely tough, does not drip easily, dries quickly and can be used to achieve many different effects, from hazy spatters to solid colours.

Fabric paints and dyes are made specially for clothes and other fabric items which need frequent washing. Use for areas of dense, flat colour rather than for the more subtle effects that can be created with spray paint. Do not use ordinary paint thinners with fabric paint, but buy its own thinner, known as 'extender'.

Bronze powders are fine metallic powders of different colours. They can be applied to wood and metal surfaces over a layer of tacky varnish to which they will adhere (see page 52).

Oil paints and acrylics can also be used. Oil paints are particularly effective on certain fabrics such as velvet (see page 52). Thin with linseed oil before use.

Masks Disposable masks, from chemists and wherever you buy spray paint, should be worn when you are using aerosols for large areas, to prevent you inhaling the fine spray.

Brushes Blunt-ended stipple brushes should vary in size according to the stencil pattern: 12 mm ($\frac{1}{2}$ in) and 40 mm ($1\frac{1}{2}$ in) are the most useful. A very fine paint-brush may also be useful for outlining the stencil pattern if its edges are uneven. Sponges and pieces of velvet or flannel can also be used to apply paint; velvet must be used, wrapped round a forefinger, to apply bronze powders to a tacky surface.

Adhesives To attach a stencil to the surface to be painted, you will need masking tape or another easily removable adhesive such as Blu-tak or Buddies, and, for surfaces where the paint is likely to drip or run under the masked area, dressmaker's pins to attach round the edges of the cut-out area. Alternatively, for walls you can spray the back of the stencil all over with an aerosol adhesive such as Spray Mount, which gives excellent results (preventing paint going behind the stencil paper) and comes off easily without damaging the wall surface.

Making your own stencils

First choose a design (perhaps from pages 56–7 or from a magazine or a book of stencil designs) or create your own – see below – and trace it on to commercially prepared oiled stencil paper. Alternatively, turn a page of the book with your chosen design into a waterproof stencil by painting both sides of the page with a layer of polyurethane varnish. If the pattern has very large areas to be coloured, they must be divided by linking pieces to hold the stencil together. To cut out the design, anchor the paper to a cutting board with masking tape and use a craft knife or scalpel to cut round the motifs, keeping the blade straight rather than at an angle to the paper (1).

Creating your own designs

With practice you can create your own stencil designs. Inspiration can come from many different sources, such as wallpaper patterns, flowers, leaves and other natural objects, and motifs seen in books or magazines. To work out your design, experiment with your chosen motif on a sheet of scrap paper or newspaper. For a symmetrical design, try folding the paper in two or four before cutting it out, or fold the paper like a concertina and cut shapes which repeat themselves when the folds are opened out (2). Make fairly simple designs at first.

Trace over the design in pencil. Then decide which parts are to be transferred and coloured, that is, those areas which are to be cut out from the final stencil. Shade these parts with pencil to help you visualize the design. Experiment by repeating and reversing a single stencil to make pairs or borders for curtains or a wall frieze (3).

How to use stencils

To decorate walls

Any smooth wall, outdoors or in, papered or not, can make a good surface for stencils, using spray paint. Although the method is simple the results can be spectacular. Outside, a trellis of flowers on the walls of a house or flat, perhaps in a roof garden or balcony, or two flowering trees in pots on either side of your front door, can brighten up city living even if you have no garden. Other ideas include a 'fresco' look for indoor walls, which can be achieved by stencilling on newly dried plaster using red oxide (car paint undercoat which also comes in aerosol cans). When dry, this can be rubbed lightly with fine sandpaper to give a very subtle matt effect.

Wall stencils can also be used to make a frieze round the top of a room, used as borders round doors and windows, or dotted about the walls at random.

Surfaces to be stencilled should be clean, dry and free from grease. Remove any grime by sponging with a weak solution of detergent. If the wall is in a poor state and you need to apply a fresh coat of paint, use matt emulsion, except in bathrooms and kitchens, where tougher paints such as silk emulsion or gloss should be used.

It is extremely important to practise using the spray paint before starting on a project, particularly if you want subtle and delicate effects. Build up the colour with several very faint layers rather than with one layer of solid colour.

You will need: stencils; tailor's chalk; tape-measure or ruler; masking tape; dressmaker's pins (but if your wall is concrete or the stencil plastic, use easily removable adhesives such as Blu-tak or Buddies); sheets of newspaper; spray paints in various colours; turpentine or white spirit; clear polyurethane varnish (optional); scissors.

Method

First decide where you will place the design and, for repeats, measure the wall carefully and mark the position of each repeat with tailor's chalk.

Fix the stencil in place with masking tape, then gently tap dressmaker's pins through the stencil into the wall so that the stencil lies flat against the wall. To prevent accidents, fix pieces of newspaper to the surrounding wall with masking tape.

Plan which areas of the design you want to spray with which colour, and mask off with newspaper all parts of the pattern not yet to be sprayed. For example, on a design with flowers and leaves, first mask off the flowers and spray all the leaves. When the leaves are dry, mask them off, then uncover the flowers and spray them. For subtle tonal effects, use two or three shades of the same colour for each part of the pattern, and spray each one very lightly (4) so that the effect is pointillist, that is, composed of hundreds of tiny dots of colour. It does not matter if differently coloured areas merge together at their edges, as long as the paint is very lightly sprayed.

When all the paint is completely dry, remove the stencil and clean it with turpentine or white spirit. (Make sure that the stencil is dry before using it again.)

Car spray paint is very tough and the stencilled design will not require extra protection. However, it may be advisable to seal the whole wall with a coat of clear polyurethane varnish if the design is likely to be knocked and perhaps chipped.

These three photographs all show the
beautiful effects that can be achieved by using
cans of spray paint for stencilling. The paint
is available in hundreds of mellow colours,
and several shades of a colour, used together
in the same part of a design, will give subtle
tonal gradations. Different colours can be
merged together where they meet in the
design – this is not only easier to do but looks
much better than hard-edged changes of
colour. Always spray very lightly in short
bursts for a soft effect. The designs shown in
the bedroom (below and far right) are all part
of a set of ready-cut stencils available
commercially, while the pot of daisies (right)
is an example of a hand-cut stencil.

When stencilling a frieze round the walls of
a room, you may have difficulty in fitting the
design to the corners. Start from the middle of
each wall, working outwards towards the
corners which should be left until the end,
when you may need to cut the stencil so that
the design fits the angle of the two walls
satisfactorily. If this cut stencil does not fit
the other corners, stick it together with
masking tape, fit it to another corner and cut
again as required. As an alternative, if the
corners do not match exactly you can always
fill in the spaces with smaller parts of the
design. The same applies to stencils as border
designs on floors.

To decorate metal

Metal is the ideal surface for stencilling with cellulose spray paint. By this method, everyday objects such as washing machines, fridges, cookers, dustbins and even cars can be transformed into colourful and decorative items that are fun to live with.

Having prepared the surface to be stencilled by sanding it down and applying a rust inhibitor if necessary, give it a background coat of spray paint. When this is dry, simply fix the stencil to the surface with magnets (children's toy magnets are ideal) or pieces of Blu-tak or Buddies, and apply spray paint as for wall stencilling (see page 49).

Bronze stencilling

Another stencilling method which lends itself to metal surfaces is bronze stencilling. Here, fine metallic powders, called 'bronze' powders (available in different shades from artist's suppliers and crafts shops), are applied through the cut-out areas of the stencil (which have already been made tacky with a coat of varnish to which the powders will adhere). Fairly small metal household objects which demand quite subtle or delicate patterns are most suitable; wastepaper bins, storage tins, trays, plates, mugs and even old cans for use as pencil jars or vases can be decorated effectively in this way.

You will need: fine sandpaper; rust inhibitor such as Jenolite; can of spray paint; sable or camel-hair paintbrush; polyurethane varnish; bronze powders; pieces of velvet about 100 mm (4 in) square (one more than the number of powder colours); .000 gauge steel wool; lint-free cloth; stencils.

Method
First, make sure that the metal surface is free from rust by sanding any 'bubbly' areas and, if necessary, applying a rust inhibitor; then apply a coat of spray paint to the whole surface of the object. Allow to dry.

Paint the whole area to be stencilled with a thin coat of varnish. Touch it lightly with the fingertips from time to time, and when it remains tacky to the touch but no longer comes off on the fingers, the surface is ready for stencilling. (The time between varnishing and stencilling will vary with the air temperature and type of varnish.)

Pour a small amount of each of the different coloured bronze powders in separate heaps on a work surface. Place a piece of velvet next to each heap. Position the stencil on the tacky surface: the

adhesive qualities of the varnish should keep it in place, although with a curved surface (such as the sides of a round biscuit tin) you will probably have to tape the stencil in position.

Wrap a piece of velvet round your forefinger and dip it into one of the mounds of colour. Apply this to the tacky surface showing through the stencil with a light but firm rubbing movement (1), taking care not to move the stencil which will blur the edges of the design.

When all the powders have been applied, rub the design with a clean piece of velvet to remove any loose particles of powder; this will stop the powder spreading when you apply the final coat of varnish. Remove the stencil and let the varnish harden and dry completely, then rub the entire surface lightly with .000 gauge steel wool. Polish with a lint-free cloth before applying a final coat of varnish.

To decorate fabric

Cotton, linen, velvet and silk are the fabrics which best accept sprayed-on stencils. A loosely woven or rough fibre like hessian is too 'grainy' for spray-stencilling, and most synthetics will not take fabric paint or dye successfully. If you are not sure of the fibre content of the item you wish to stencil, test a sample with the paint or dye to see whether it 'takes'.

Cellulose spray paint, used in the same way as on walls (see the photographs on pages 50–1), is hand-washable but should be washed separately and will fade slightly. Paint specially made for fabric, such as Dylon Color Fun, has the advantage of being colour-fast but is less easy to use. Fabric dyes available in paste form are a simpler medium for most fabrics. Oil paint is particularly effective on velvet, giving a rich result (see below). However, it takes a long time to dry: oil-stencilled velvet should be left in a warm place for about six weeks before use.

Oil stencilling on velvet

Oil-stencilled velvet can be used to make a pretty tea-cosy (see pages 54–5), an old-fashioned firescreen, or even something larger such as curtains. To create the antique cream shade of velvet so beloved of the Victorians and traditional for this type of stencilling, simply soak as much white velvet as you need in a lukewarm solution of two teabags to 4.5 litres (1 gal) of water for a few minutes. Then lay the fabric flat on a draining board, push your hands across it to force the water through it (**2**), and leave to dry. The oil paints should not be used direct from the tube, but mixed on a makeshift palette (a saucer will do) and diluted slightly with linseed oil.

You will need: a piece of prepared cream velvet of the desired shape and size (for a tea-cosy, cut two equal pieces of the dimensions of a bought padded inner cosy); stiff card slightly larger than the area of the stencil; masking tape; stencil; tubes of oil paint in the colours of your choice (pinks, blues and green were used for the cosy shown on pages 54–5); linseed oil; a 10 mm ($\frac{1}{2}$ in) stipple brush or several 10 cm (4 in) squares of flannel; a fine paintbrush.

Method

Place the velvet, right side up, over the card so that the area you wish to stencil is centrally positioned. Pull the fabric taut and tape it to the card. Fix the stencil to the top of the velvet with masking tape.

Mix and thin the oil paints with a little linseed oil, and apply them to the fabric through the stencil with a stipple brush or a piece of flannel wrapped round your forefinger. Use a very small amount of paint and dab it on the velvet lightly, to prevent a caked effect when it dries (**3**).

About ten minutes after applying the main colours, use a fine brush to apply finishing touches such as leaf veins, if you wish. Remove the stencil and neaten any rough edges with the brush (**4**).

To decorate mirrors and glass

Using spray paint, the technique is similar to stencilling on walls (see page 49), but since glass is non-porous and even the slightest excess of paint will cause the stencil to 'dribble', care must be taken to spray as lightly as possible: place the item to be stencilled on a flat surface if you can. To keep the stencil in place and prevent the paint dribbling under it, use Spray Mount to stick it to the mirror.

bronze stencilling

1

oil stencilling

2

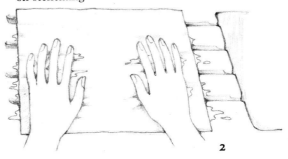

3

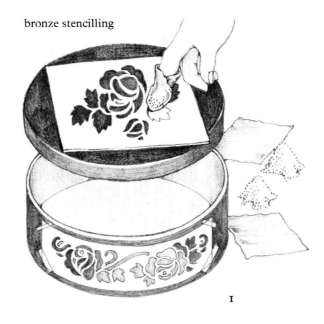

4

Enliven teatime with pretty handmade stencil designs (left). The old biscuit tin was revitalized with a coat of spray paint followed by the application of bronze powders through the stencil, while the pattern on the tea-cosy was applied with oil paints to a piece of specially dyed velvet which was then made up into a cover to fit a padded inner cosy (all instructions on page 52).

A cheap cane blind (top) is another surface that can be transformed with a few cans of spray paint, while the plain clutch bag (above) has been lifted out of the ordinary with a delicate stencil pattern, using fabric dye applied with a stipple brush.

Stencilling on wood

To stencil a wooden surface, whether it is a piece of furniture like a table or the cupboard pictured on pages 46–7, a large area such as a floor or a small household item like a tray, no special preparation is necessary beyond that required for ordinary painting. The wood must be clean and completely free from grease; any oily patches should be removed with detergent. If the existing paint on the object to be stencilled is worn and scratched but a pleasing colour, there is no need to remove it completely: after cleaning and sanding it with fine sandpaper, it can be sprayed extremely lightly all over, in a shade as close as possible to the original colour. This use of spray paint gives a most subtle effect and works very well as a base for stencils.

Once the surface has been prepared, the stencils can be fixed in position and the colours applied. Aerosol cans of spray paint should be sprayed on in short bursts, as described for walls (see page 49). If you are using artist's acrylic colour, apply it with a small stencil brush and use the paint sparingly. Bronze powders can also be used on wood: the sanded surface should be sealed with clear polyurethane varnish and the powders applied when the varnish is still tacky, in the same way as for metal surfaces (see page 52).

After stencilling wood you may wish to seal the surface. The cupboard shown on page 46 was simply polished with beeswax, and any clear wax polish will produce a smooth, mellow effect; but you could use a clear lacquer or glaze such as Fend for a somewhat tougher finish, say for a table or dresser withstanding heavier use. A wooden floor, however, needs to be sealed with several coats of clear polyurethane varnish, as floors take so much wear and tear that the design must be well protected from possible chipping. Matt polyurethane is the best type to use if you do not want it to show or be shiny.

Stencilling on paper

Most paper objects are small enough to be laid flat, which makes paper a very easy surface to stencil. Items such as kites, writing paper and envelopes, greetings cards and matching wrapping paper and gift tags are all good subjects for stencilling. Spray paint and any other paint which can usually be applied to paper – such as watercolour – can be used. Use slightly absorbent paper if possible, and keep the design simple, particularly on ephemeral items. Fix the stencil to the paper with masking tape or pins, and apply the colour using the techniques already described in this chapter.

tea-cosy

biscuit tin

The stencil designs shown here have been used to decorate some of the items illustrated on the previous pages. They can simply be traced off and transferred to stencil paper (see page 93 for information on transferring designs), and applied to walls, floors, fabrics and household objects of all kinds.

bag

blind

Modelled & painted flowers

Self-hardening clays that do not require firing mean that you can do all kinds of modelling at home with the minimum of equipment. Attractive and inexpensive china ornaments, such as this decorated Victorian-style mirror, and pretty jewellery like the comb, the brooches and the pansy pendant shown here can easily be made using the instructions on the following pages. Much of the beauty of these china flowers lies in their subtle colours, and you can achieve these attractive effects by using the simple painting techniques described in the projects. Enamel paint, or matt paint plus a coat of varnish, will give the flowers a ceramic-like glaze.

If you enjoy painting but don't have the time or nimble enough fingers for modelling, there's another way of producing beautiful china flowers at a fraction of the cost of buying fine porcelain ones. Simply by coating ordinary plastic flowers with enamel paint (see page 69) you can make them seem remarkably like the real thing, and they look particularly good in massed arrangements like the ones shown on pages 66–7.

Tools & materials

Self-hardening clay Makes such as DAS or Harbutt's Plastone come ready to use in air-tight packets. Read the maker's instructions carefully and practise handling the clay before you start on a project, so that you have an idea of the amount required and can get used to its texture and flexibility (which vary according to the make). Keep your fingers moist as you work, to prevent the clay from drying out, and if you have to stop halfway through a project wrap the unfinished piece in a damp cloth so that it remains workable. The clay will set hard in about twenty-four hours but it is advisable to leave it for at least thirty-six hours before painting. Reseal the remaining clay in the packet after use so that it retains pliability.

Plastic modelling tools Invaluable modelling aids, these have ends which may be straight, curved, pointed, serrated or spatula-shaped, and they are particularly useful for joining delicate pieces of clay and for making interesting patterns on its surface.

White, magnolia or cream matt vinyl emulsion Available in very small tins of 125 ml ($\frac{1}{4}$ pint), this should be used as a preparatory coat before matt colours are applied to clay, as it prevents them merging with the grey of the clay. This size tin will last a long time as so little is needed for each flower. Buy matt emulsion, not silk which will not take water-based paint. Allow two to three hours for it to dry.

Poster paint Available in small jars in a wide range of colours, the matt finish is very effective, as the colours can be worked into each other to give subtle tones and shading.

Designer's gouache This is like poster paint but available in tubes. Use the matt finish as it enables you to achieve fine gradations of colour.

Enamel paint Its hard, bright finish makes enamel suitable for clay objects requiring a bold effect, and also for plastic flowers, but not for articles which depend on subtlety of colouring. It does not require varnishing.

Matt enamel varnish Apply sparingly over flat paint for a ceramic effect.

Brushes Sable brushes are best; use size 0 for delicate work such as painting jewellery.

Adhesive Use clear adhesive such as Uhu to stick a finished item to a surface such as a brooch clasp.

Making the basic shapes

The basic shapes described below can be used to make all kinds of jewellery, not just the pieces shown in this chapter. And you can also use them to decorate items such as the mirror described on page 64, or a picture frame, but remember that the thin petals are quite fragile.

After making the shapes leave them to dry for at least thirty-six hours before assembling or painting; do not attempt to move them until they are set hard, as the shapes could be distorted.

To make a pansy Take a small piece of clay and roll it into a ball about the size of a pea. Continue rolling one end of the ball to a point, so that it is bullet-shaped (**1**).

Holding the pointed end of the 'bullet' between the thumb and forefinger of one hand, use the thumb and forefinger of the other to press the rest of the ball out as a petal shape (**2** and **3**).

With the flat petal in one hand, squeeze the pointed end to gather it up, forming a small pleat (**4**). Make five petals like this (**5**) and set them aside.

Now make the flat base to which the petals will be anchored. Take a slightly larger ball of clay and press it out to form a disc, place it on the work surface and neaten the edges with a modelling tool so that the disc is circular.

Take the first petal and, using a modelling tool, press the pleated end of the petal into the centre of the disc (**6**). Repeat with all five petals, overlapping each one slightly (**7**) to form the flower.

To make the pansy centre, take a tiny ball of clay and press it on to the middle of the flower, covering the area where the petals join. With the pointed end of a modelling tool, pierce small holes in the centre for decorative effect (**8**).

To make a periwinkle Follow figures 1–3 for the pansy to make five flat petal shapes. Hold each petal by the pointed end and squeeze the two rounded corners together (**9**) to form a pleat on the outer edge of the petal (**10**).

Continue in exactly the same way as for the pansy (figures 6–8), or make a different decorative centre by following figure 14 (below).

To make a daisy Begin exactly as if you were making a pansy (figures 1–3). Hold the petal by the round end and squeeze the edges on either side of the pointed end so that they meet to form a cone shape (**11**).

Make the next petal and, using a modelling tool, join it to the first petal at the pointed end, with the petals lying close to each other and the cone shape facing upwards. Make four more petals in the same way, joining the pointed end of each one to the previous petal as you make it (**12**). Do not try to join the petals by hand alone; a modelling tool is essential for guiding the pointed ends of the petals together, since they have no supporting disc behind them.

To make the flower-head rigid despite not having a supporting disc, pinch the outer, rounded corners of adjoining petals together (**13**).

To make the daisy centre, make three or four minuscule balls of clay (about the size of pinheads) and, using a modelling tool, guide them into the centre of the flower. Pierce a hole in the middle of each one (**14**).

To make a rose Begin by following figure 1 for the pansy, to make a bullet shape. Set it aside. Roll another small piece of clay into a ball and flatten it between thumb and forefinger to make an oval shape. Gently stretch the oval shape sideways between thumb and forefinger to form a wide petal shape (**15**).

To form the rose centre, place the bullet-shaped piece of clay on the petal, its pointed end projecting just beyond the bottom edge of the petal. Wrap the petal round the bullet shape, one side at a time (**16**) so that the sides overlap.

Take a slightly larger piece of clay and make another wide petal shape. Place the rose centre on this second petal (**17**) so that the petal projects a little beyond it at the top, and position it so that the second petal overlaps in a different place from the first when wrapped round it (**18**).

Make and attach more petals in the same way, using a slightly larger piece of clay each time. A cone shape, growing gradually wider at the top, will be formed. For a rosebud use only three or four petals (**19**). A full-blown rose can be made with as many petals as you like; stretch the upper edges of the last few petals with thumb and forefinger so that they curve outwards (**20**).

To make a leaf Roll a piece of clay into a ball, then roll it between thumb and forefinger so that the ball elongates. Roll both ends until they are slightly pointed (**21**). Flatten the fatter central section, tapering it to the pointed ends to make a leaf shape (**22**).

To make it look more realistic (while the clay is still of modelling consistency) you can press the underside of a real rose leaf gently on to it. When you pull away the real leaf you will see an impressed pattern of veins on the clay (**23**). Taking care not to smudge the 'veins', bend the leaf to the desired angle.

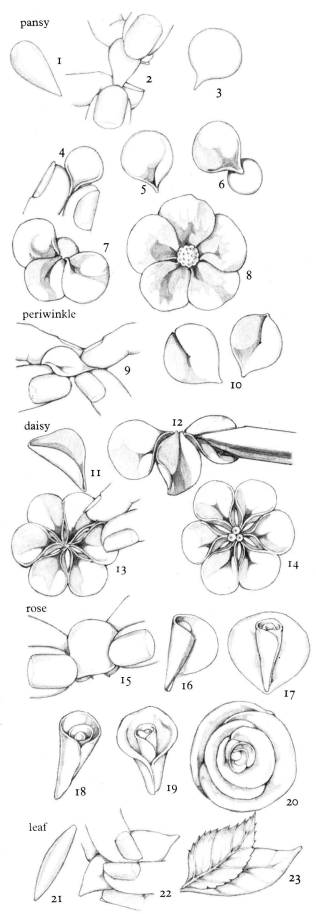

This pretty long-stemmed flower brooch (left) could be made using either the basic pansy, the periwinkle or the daisy shape; and a variation of this style is shown in the photograph on pages 58–9. Attached to the flower-head are several thin stem shapes laid together, with one of them twisted round the others. This not only creates a more interesting shape for a piece of jewellery than a single stem, but makes the brooch stronger. While still damp, the stems can be twisted in various ways until you find a pleasing shape. For full instructions, see page 65.

These colourful hair slides (above) are simple variations on the flower theme. As slides are usually long and narrow it is difficult to make realistic flowers for them, but single petals rather than whole flower-heads make an effective decoration. Choose any type of flower – pansy, daisy or periwinkle – and make two small petals slightly wider than the slide. Make two even smaller petals of the

same design and two decorative centres. Fix each smaller petal inside each larger one and finish off with the centres placed over the joined ends of the petals.

When the petals are dry, glue them in position with a clear adhesive such as Uhu, wait until set, then coat with emulsion paint. They can then be painted with designer's gouache in colours to complement the slide. As the flowers are rather small it is best to use just one colour per flower, rather than shading the petals. When the paint is dry (after about two or three hours), finish them off with a coat of varnish.

Other flower decorations for the hair include the comb shown on page 59. For one comb, make one or two complete flowers of your choice (periwinkles are probably the simplest) and an even number of half flowers of just three petals each, making sure that their size will fit the comb. The supporting disc at the base of each flower can then be covered with a decorative centre.

Mirror

Although any mirror can be made more interesting with the addition of clay flowers, the ideal kind to use is an old one which was once decorated in this way, as it will already have a shaped backing board on to which the flowers can be fixed. Such mirrors, normally circular, can frequently be found in second-hand shops with the original decoration chipped and broken. If you are not lucky enough to find one, you will either have to make a shaped back from hardboard or plywood (see below), or stick the clay directly on to the mirror.

You will need: modelling and painting equipment (see page 60); a small chisel or screwdriver; a sheet of tracing paper; a rolling pin or bottle; a pencil; a sharp craft knife; epoxy resin adhesive such as Araldite; clear adhesive; fine sandpaper.

Method
Working on an old mirror, use a chisel or screwdriver to prise away any remaining plaster flowers from the projection or overhang at the top of the mirror (**1**). Rub the surface smooth with fine sandpaper.

If you are working with a modern mirror and have to back it yourself, choose a square shape, as a curved back needs a little more wood-working skill and equipment. Measure the mirror and make a hardboard or plywood back which fits exactly at the bottom and sides but has a shaped overhang at the top on which to put the flowers. Stick the back to the mirror with epoxy resin adhesive.

To make a clay base for the flowers, first place the tracing paper over the area of the overhang and trace the edges of the shape with a pencil. Now form a large lump of clay into a sausage shape, then roll it out to a thickness of 4 mm ($\frac{1}{8}$ in) and large enough to cover the overhang.

Lay the tracing paper on the clay, press down on the pencil line with the pointed end of a modelling tool to impress the shape on the clay, then lift the paper. Cut out the shape along this line with a sharp knife (putting back the excess clay in its bag for further use). Leave the shaped clay on the work surface until it is completely hard, then stick it on to the wooden overhang (**2**) with an epoxy resin adhesive (or stick it directly on the mirror if it has no overhang). Sandpaper any rough edges smooth.

To decorate the mirror, either sketch out a design first and make flowers to fit, or simply create a number of different flowers with which to construct an arrangement. Stems and leaves can then be fitted round them to fill gaps and make the design 'flow'. Make the flowers following the instructions on pages 60–1. All flowers must be completely dry before being stuck in position. For artistic effect make a dominant feature of the central flower or flowers, and work from the centre outwards, gluing the largest flowers first with clear adhesive (**3**).

Paint the emulsion base coat very sparingly (see page 60) so as not to fill in any fine detail. If the design is rather fussy, as here (see also page 58), it is best to paint each flower one flat pastel colour rather than attempting complicated shading. Finally, varnish all the painted surfaces and leave to dry.

Long-stemmed brooch

You will need: modelling clay and tools (see page 60); matt vinyl emulsion; a sable paintbrush, size 0; designer's gouache in suitable colours; matt enamel varnish; a round metal brooch fitting 2 cm ($\frac{3}{4}$ in) in diameter; clear adhesive.

Method

Make one of the flower-heads described on pages 60–1, ensuring that its clay disc base is the same size as the brooch fitting. Do not worry if it dries a little while you make the stem and leaves; if it is firm when the other parts are attached it will not lose its shape.

To make the stem (this brooch has a long, decorative multi-stem) roll out five very thin sausage shapes all the same length and join them together at the top by squeezing them together. While the clay is still pliable, twist one of the stems lightly round the others (**1**).

Make two leaves as described on page 61, either gently curved to fit round the flower-head (**2**) or smaller and wider for a daisy or periwinkle, with vein markings, and attach them just below the flower-head, or along the stem (**3** and **4**).

To assemble the brooch (**5**), dampen the back of the flower disc (with a small wet paintbrush) and use a modelling tool to press the top end of the stem and the tops of the leaves gently into position on the back of the disc. Make another disc the same size as the one already on the flower back. Dampen the original disc again and place the new disc on top of it, covering the stem tops. Press the edges of the two discs together with a modelling tool. Set aside to dry thoroughly, then attach the brooch fitting to the back of the flower-head with clear adhesive.

To paint the brooch, first apply a base coat of matt vinyl emulsion (making sure that the holes in the flower centre do not fill up), and allow to dry. Always hold the brooch by the fastener so that there is no fear of smudging previously painted areas, and paint the stems and leaves first. Use your imagination when colouring the petals; the brooch shown on page 62 has a strong colour at the centre of the petals fading towards the edges, but it could be the other way round. (Mix the gouache thoroughly if you are combining colours from different tubes.) Finish by painting the flower centre, and leave to dry.

Finally, apply matt varnish sparingly over all the painted surfaces of the brooch, and leave to dry for at least thirty-six hours.

Enamel-painted plastic flowers look just like porcelain ones, especially when they are boldly arranged in vases or hanging baskets. You can mix them with dried hydrangeas, lavender and other real flowers for an informal effect (left), or arrange them in a simpler, more traditional fashion for a table centre-piece (top). Instructions on page 69.

Round and oblong beads with floral designs (shown above with a selection of paints and modelling tools) are simple to make with self-hardening clay, painted in bright colours and varnished. Instructions on page 69.

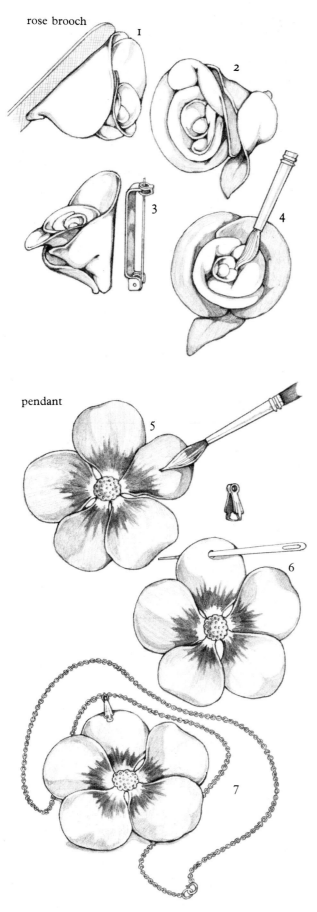

rose brooch

pendant

Rose brooch

You will need: modelling clay and tools; matt vinyl emulsion; gouache in white, green and red; varnish; an emery board; an oblong brooch fitting; adhesive.

Method
Make a full-blown rose (page 61, figure 20), ensuring that the back of the last outer petal has a flat surface to which the fitting can be attached. Leave to dry, then use an emery board on the flat back to rub off any excess clay, and also on the stem end of the rose, where the leaf will be attached (**1**).

Make a leaf (page 61), then use a wet paintbrush to dampen the stem end of the rose and attach the leaf at this point (**2**). Leave to dry.

Glue the fastener to the back of the brooch (**3**), then apply a base coat of matt emulsion paint to the clay (see page 60). Mix the white and red paint and paint the outer two or three petals. Add a little more white to this colour and paint the next few petals. Continue adding white in this way until all the petals have been painted, so that the rose is paler towards the centre (**4**). Paint the leaf, leave to dry, then varnish all the painted surfaces sparingly and allow to dry for thirty-six hours.

Pendant

You will need: the same tools and materials as for the long-stemmed brooch; a metal pendant attachment and chain; a sewing or darning needle (to make the hole for the hanging device).

Method
Make one of the flowers (pages 60–1), but larger than for a brooch, say about 4 cm ($1\frac{1}{2}$ in) in diameter, and allow to dry in the usual way.

Apply the base coat of matt emulsion paint then, working with the basic colour, begin painting the central parts of the petals. Change the colour slightly, say to a darker shade, and paint about a third of the way up the petals, finishing off with the main shade again. Just before the paint dries, take a dampened paintbrush and blend the two colours into each other for a natural effect (**5**).

When the paint is completely dry, make a hole close to the edge of one petal with a needle. Gently but firmly twist the needle from side to side in the hole to make it big enough for the attachment (**6**), which is then fitted. Varnish the flower, then leave it to dry as usual before attaching the chain (**7**).

Bead necklace

These brightly coloured beads in bold shapes are painted with flower motifs in enamel paints (photograph on page 67).

You will need: the modelling equipment listed on page 60; tins of enamel paint such as Humbrol; a darning needle; a sharp craft knife; used matchsticks; leather thonging, ribbon or crochet cotton and an appropriate threading needle.

Method
For round beads, roll one piece of clay into a ball about the size of a marble, two more pieces into slightly smaller balls the same size as each other, then two or three more pairs, each pair smaller than the previous one. Set aside for half an hour.

For oblong beads, roll a piece of clay into a sausage shape and continue rolling until it is as thick as the beads you require. Use a sharp knife to cut through the sausage length at equal intervals to make four oblong beads. Set aside for half an hour.

The beads will now have set a little so that they are firmer to the touch and do not lose their shape when handled. Make holes in them by pushing a damp needle through each bead, first from one direction and then the other (1). Do this several times until the hole is large enough to take your chosen thread. Press the beads back into shape if necessary and leave to dry.

In the meantime, take a matchstick for each bead and use a knife to sharpen them all at one end. When the clay is completely dry, wedge a matchstick into the hole in each bead, so that you have something to hold while you paint them. Put a spare lump of clay on the work surface. As you paint the beads (emulsion coat first) push the matchsticks holding them into it, and leave them to dry (2).

Take the first bead, with its matchstick, from the clay base and paint it all over with one colour. Replace the matchstick in the hole in the clay from which it came and leave to dry for at least six hours. Repeat with the rest of the beads.

Using a contrasting colour, take each bead in turn and paint petal shapes on it: a single brush stroke will leave a bold petal-like shape (3). Return each bead to its place in the clay base as it is painted.

When the beads are completely dry they can be threaded: arrange the beads so that the round ones graduate in size from the central large one, with oblong ones between them or at each end (4).

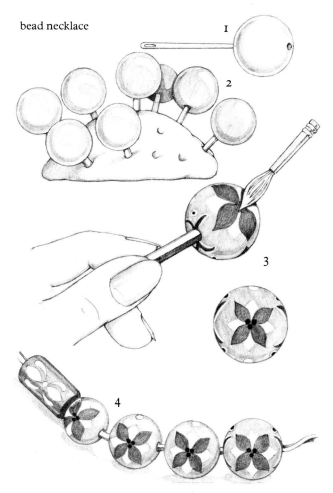

bead necklace

Enamel-painted flowers

Real china flowers are expensive, but you can easily make your own from plastic ones. Buy the smallest flowers you can find, as these are more likely to look like porcelain when painted.

You will need: several small paintbrushes; tins of enamel paint such as Humbrol, including one large tin of white enamel; plastic flowers.

Method
Simply mix the enamels until you have shades of colour which appeal to you. Mix plenty of white paint with every colour, as the white in the paint suggests that the flowers have a china base.

There is no need to paint the leaves or stalks of the flowers if they are small, as they will probably look even more like plastic when painted. But do paint the leaves of larger flowers if you are using these to make a more stylized, less delicate arrangement. In all cases, the flowers are secured in blocks of green florist's foam, in the same way as for live flower arrangements.

Paper flowers

Subtle or startling, delicate or vividly coloured, paper flowers are one of the simplest ways to brighten dark corners, impart interest to a table setting and add a pretty decorative touch to a gift wrapping. As well as being easy and fun to make, paper flowers are cheap: crêpe paper and wire are the only main ingredients needed, and you will probably find that you already have the equipment required at home, which will save you the expense of having to buy special tools.

On the following pages the methods of making the four different types of flower pictured on the left are described in detail; they are made either with one long strip of paper or using simple petal- and leaf-shaped patterns. All of them are based on garden flowers and include such realistic details as stamens, sepals and calyx, as well as petals, stems and leaves. Other kinds of flower can also be made by altering the shape or size of the patterns given in this chapter, using unusual colour combinations, or by adding different centres and leaves. And you can create your own flowers, either by carefully observing real ones and noting their main features, perhaps using real petals as templates, or by using your imagination to make more stylized designs.

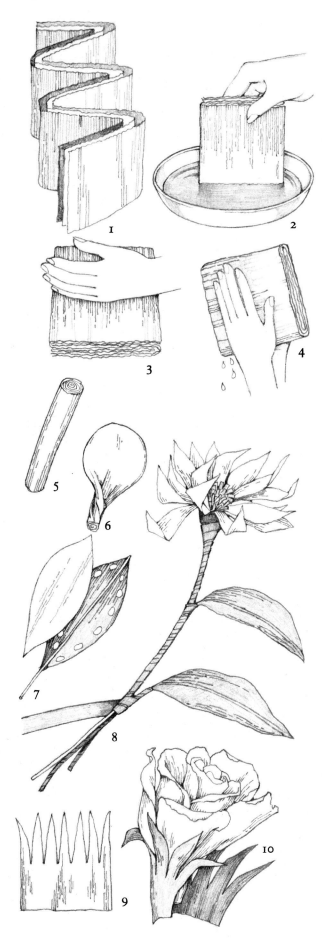

Creating natural effects

Part of the attraction of using crêpe paper to make flowers is that it is possible to reflect nature very closely. In addition, lifelike leaves, stems and centres are as important to the overall effect as beautiful petals, and paper flowers can contain all the parts of the real flower on which it is modelled (see page 8); these parts should be as delicate as you can make them. Having looked closely at flowering plants, you may think it impossible to recreate stamens with their yellow pollen or a bulbous calyx with its pointed sepals, but you will be surprised at how effective you can make these, using the simplest materials and methods.

Shading paper

To create the most natural effects in paper flowers, the paper from which their petals are made should usually show subtle gradations of colour, just like those of real flowers. The method of doing this is simple: by wetting the paper before you start, its flat colour will run and create variations in shading. If two or three papers of complementary colours are wetted and then squeezed together, the colours from each paper will run into one another to create interesting shaded effects in all of them. For example, to prepare pink shaded paper (perhaps for an arrangement of roses) combine folds of red, pink and white crêpe paper; for deep orange shading to cream, use orange, yellow and white paper; for purple, choose red, blue and mauve, and so on. Wetting and then drying the paper also have the effect of giving paper a slightly wrinkled, natural looking surface.

Make sure that you prepare enough paper for as many flowers as you will need for one project, for example, in an arrangement of roses where you want the colours to go together well. Do not unfold the crêpe paper but cut through its folds. Cut widths of 10 cm (4 in) for most flowers, especially for those made from gathering up a single strip (see pages 76–7), so that you can cut five of these strips from one fold of paper. When opened out, each strip will measure about 3 m (10 ft) long, enough for two or three flowers.

Interleave the folded lengths of paper together (1), then, holding their edges level, dip their cut edge in a shallow bowl of water about 12 mm ($\frac{1}{2}$ in) deep (2), and allow the water to seep about halfway up the paper. Place the pieces flat (still interleaved) on a draining board and use the side of your hand to press the water out, using a chopping motion and gradually working from the middle to the edge of the paper (3).

Tools & materials

Paper Crêpe paper, which makes the most successful and attractive paper flowers, comes folded in packets, called folds, in lengths of about 3 m (10 ft) when unfolded, and 50 cm (20 in) wide. It stretches very easily to at least one and a half times its original length, and can be manipulated into all kinds of shapes. This means that it can be curved and curled into petals, and wrapped round lengths of wire to make stems. It should always be stretched and cut lengthways, across the grain. You will often find that many types of flower demand that you cut right through all the folded layers of paper at once, to make a long strip.

Crêpe paper comes in many different colours, some of which are ideal just as they are for certain types of flower but, in general, shaded and blended colours which reflect nature more effectively are to be preferred. To prepare shaded paper, see page 72.

Wire There are two main types of wire needed for most paper flowers, a thin one for joining different parts of the flower and holding the flower-head together at the base, and a thicker one for making stems. Florist's stub wire, available in different gauges (widths) is useful for stems (see also page 8), but you could use galvanized wire, obtainable in reels from hardware and hobby shops, instead. Fine silver reel wire (from florist's) or electrical fuse wire is best for binding petals together.

Crumpled wire netting (chicken wire) is required for supporting the finished flowers in large arrangements, swags and garlands (see pages 78–9).

Stamens Ready-made stamens, usually of soft, fine, thread-covered wire with coloured or pearl-like bulbous ends, come in packets and are obtainable from hobby shops. You can also make your own stamens for larger or less delicate flowers, using pipe cleaners or cotton-wool buds dipped in yellow paint. Stamens can also be made from lengths of sisal twine separated into strands, and from pieces of crêpe paper with one end cut into a fringe, the other end twisted.

Wire cutters or pliers These are useful for bending wire stems to make hooks (to embed in flower-heads) as well as for actually cutting wire.

Scissors The scissors you use for cutting the paper will need to be sharp, particularly for cutting through several layers of paper at a time.

Adhesive Use a quick-drying, clear-setting PVA glue such as Unibond.

Pick up the pieces together and press them gently between both hands to finish squeezing out the water (4). This makes the colours run and blend together: for example the white paper will have streaks of the other two colours on it. Separate the pieces and leave them to dry in a warm place such as an airing cupboard before use.

To make centres, leaves, stems and sepals
Centres Many kinds of flower centre can be made, according to the type and size of the flower you are creating, and with care they can be very convincing. Pipe cleaners, for example, can be bent over at the top at different angles to make stamens for different flowers, then dipped in yellow paint so that they look as if they are covered with pollen. A short length of sisal twine or coarse string separated into strands can be treated in the same way and used for smaller or more delicate flowers. A length of crêpe paper, cut into a fringe along one side and twisted up, also makes effective stamens. Other types of centre include those made from a narrow strip of crêpe paper rolled up into a cylindrical shape (5), or a small ball of paper wrapped in another piece of paper stretched smoothly round it and twisted up at the bottom (6).

Leaves Copy the shapes and patterns of real leaves, and note how they lie in relation to the stem: some single leaves grow alternately on either side of the stem, while others grow in opposite pairs.

Leaves should be supported and strengthed by means of a length of fine wire glued between two layers of paper (7); the wire should be long enough to form a stem which can be twisted round the main stem of a flower. It can then be either wrapped in green paper as for main stems (see below), or attached so closely that it is not visible as a separate stem. Full instructions for making leaves are given on pages 80–1.

Stems Realistic stems can be made from lengths of wire (see Tools & materials) with narrow strips of green crêpe paper wound round them (8). Choose wire of a thickness to suit the size of the flower. To make a really thick stem for a heavy-headed flower such as a tulip, thread a waxed paper straw over the wire, glue it lightly to the flower-head and cover in the usual way. To make a very long, strong flower stem for a large-scale flower, bind the wire stem of the flower to a sturdy rod such as a plant support stick, using florist's tape (see page 8). You can also use natural twiggy branches for attaching several flower-heads: these should be covered with crêpe paper with flowers and leaves bound into them.

Sepals To make sepals, take a short length of green crêpe paper about 10 cm (4 in) wide and cut one side of it into points (9). Wrap this round the base of a flower-head, pointed side up, and glue in place. (10). You can vary the width and angle of the points for different effects.

The beauty of paper flowers is that they can be used in so many ways. The perfect single red rose which decorates the parcel (right) indicates that special care has been taken with the gift, and forms a lasting reminder of the occasion. You can, of course, use more than one flower in this way, in a small posy, or even make the flower itself the gift, perhaps by presenting a waxed example (see below and page 81) in a transparent box.

Waxed flowers like these (below and far right) are simply crêpe paper flowers whose heads have been dipped in molten paraffin wax. They look particularly effective arranged in china bowls or under a glass dome with plenty of light on them. They are often more natural looking than plain paper flowers because the wax gives their petals the sort of sheen that succulent flowers – stephanotis, lilies and orchids, for example – have in reality. However, waxed flowers eventually become limp and the wax can be damaged or crack if handled too much. Avoid using them as decorations to be worn – on a lapel or to trim a hat – for this reason. They can, however, be revived easily by rewaxing (see the instructions on page 81).

Roses

The roses shown on pages 70–1 are each made from a single long strip of crêpe paper. To gain a natural, shaded effect for the petals, use packets of paper in complementary colours and make several flowers, first blending the colours together (see page 72).

You will need: folded, shaded crêpe paper; green crêpe paper; florist's or galvanized wire; fine silver reel or fuse wire; wire cutters; sharp scissors; PVA glue such as Unibond.

Method

First make the petals. Hold the folded crêpe paper with its cut edges together, and cut out two equal semicircular shapes across one raw side (**1**). Unfold the paper and you will have equal petal shapes all along its length (**2**).

Only a 120 cm (4 ft) length of petals is required for one rose, so fold the crêpe paper in half and cut it in two. Working with one strip only, take a length of florist's or galvanized wire and curl the top edge of each petal around it a couple of times, always in the same direction. Do not simply turn over the edges in the straight line, but slant the wire against the paper so that the two sides of each petal curl inwards towards the centre (**3**).

With the curled edges facing away from you, gently stretch each petal across its width with fingers and thumbs, to curve the whole petal (**4**). Now roll up the strip of petals, curled edges facing outwards, holding the base of the strip firmly as you roll it (**5**). As you continue and the flower-head fills out, ensure that the petals seem to grow outwards by pleating the bottom of the strip.

Hold the finished head in one hand and wind a 10 cm (4 in) length of fine wire firmly round the base, twisting the ends together to secure them (**6**).

For the stem, take a suitable length of florist's or galvanized wire and use wire cutters to bend one end of it into a small hook. Push the straight end of the wire down through the centre of the flower (**7**) so that the hook is embedded in the centre of the petals.

Use green crêpe paper to make sepals (see page 73), then finish the stem: cut a long strip of green crêpe paper about 12 mm ($\frac{1}{2}$ in) wide, glue one end of it to the sepals and wind it tightly round the base of the flower a few times, then on down the whole length of the stem. Stretch one side of the strip as you go so that it is at an angle to the stem (**8**). At the end of the stem cut off excess paper and glue the end in place to secure it.

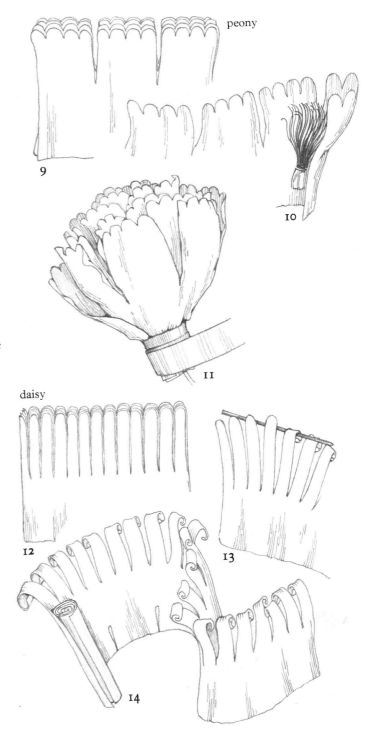

peony

9

10

11

daisy

12

13

14

Peonies

The peonies differ from the roses only in the shape of their petals; and they have stamens and no sepals.

You will need: tools and materials as described on page 73.

Method
To make the petals, hold the folded, shaded crêpe paper with its raw edges together, and mark and cut out the shape of the petals along one raw edge, as shown (**9**). Unfold the paper and stretch each petal across its width to curve it (see figure 4).

Position the stamens of your choice at one end of the strip of petals, their base aligning with the bottom edge of the paper (**10**), and roll up the petals round it (see figure 5). Bind the base of the flower-head with fine wire (see figure 6).

Make the stem from a hooked length of florist's wire inserted through the centre of the flower-head from the top (see figure 7).

Cut a long strip of green paper about 12 mm ($\frac{1}{2}$ in) wide. Glue one end of it to the base of the flower-head, wrap the strip round the base a few times to form a calyx (**11**), then bind the stem (see figure 8).

Daisies

Both large ox-eye daisies and small lawn daisies can be made in the same way, the only difference between them being that the stems of lawn daisies are made from finer wire. They are both created from one continuous strip of crêpe paper.

You will need: white, yellow and green crêpe paper, unshaded; ball-point pen; florist's or galvanized wire; silver reel or fuse wire; wire cutters; sharp scissors; PVA glue such as Unibond.

Method
Cut through the layers of a fold of white crêpe paper so that you have a strip the usual width or slightly less for an ox-eye daisy, and about 25 mm (1 in) wide for a lawn daisy. From this strip cut lengths of about 40 cm (16 in) for large daisies, 10 cm (4 in) for small ones. For one daisy, fold each length in half twice and draw up to a dozen long, thin petal shapes along one edge (**12**). Cut round the shapes and unfold the paper, then use galvanized or florist's wire to curl the tops of the petals, all in the same direction (**13**). To make the centre, cut a length of yellow crêpe paper 20 cm (8 in) by 10 cm (4 in) for a large daisy, 75 mm (3 in) by 20 mm ($\frac{3}{4}$ in) for a small one, and pull it

gently lengthways to stretch it. Fold this strip in half along its length, and roll it up tightly to form a cylinder (see figure 5 on page 73), gluing the end.

Wind the strip of petals, curved outwards, round this centre, pleating it as you go (**14**). Secure the base of the flower-head with fuse wire (see figure 6) and make a stem for an ox-eye daisy in the same way as for a rose (see figure 7). For a lawn daisy, simply wrap another length of fuse wire round the base, then twist the ends to form a stem. In both cases finish the stem with green paper (see figure 11).

Paper flowers, waxed or unwaxed, can be used to splendid effect in garlands of all kinds. For a special occasion, brighten your buffet table with a garland of colourful paper flowers looped round the sides of the cloth (left). Fasten the flowers in position with drawing pins, or sew them to the fabric. After use they can be removed from the tablecloth and stored until the next celebration. Window frames, walls, bannisters and doorways can all be adorned in this way for festive occasions; to make as big an impact with fresh flowers would be enormously expensive, and of course the flowers would wilt very quickly without water. All types of garland can be made by the same basic method: simply vary the length of the garland and the size and type of flowers to suit your purpose. Instructions for making garlands are on page 81.

Small flowers such as lawn daisies make an appealing decoration for cakes and puddings, and can be used to fill the hollow of a savarin (above), or as a garland round the base of a birthday or wedding cake. Instructions for making daisies are on page 77.

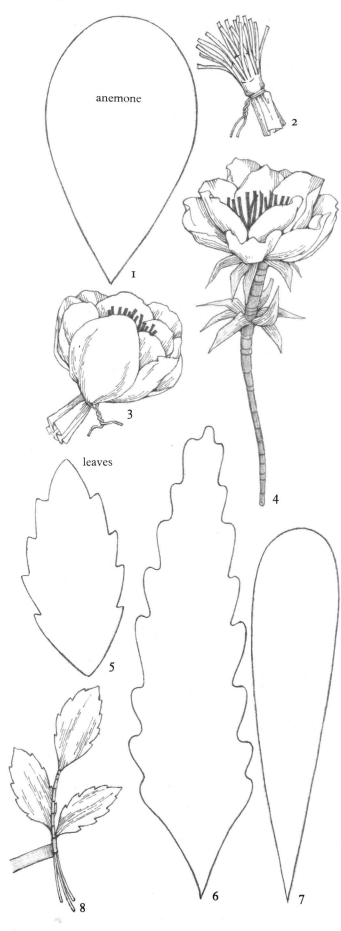

anemone

1

2

3

leaves

4

5

6

7

8

Anemones

This flower differs from all the others described in this chapter in that its petals are cut individually from a template, rather than in one long strip.

You will need: folded, shaded crêpe paper (use purples, pinks and deep red for petals); green and black crêpe paper for stem and sepals; tracing paper; and tools and equipment as for daisies.

Method

Trace off the petal shape (1) and transfer it to a piece of shaded crêpe paper, folded to give ten thicknesses. Cut round this shape, making sure that the paper's grain runs along its length, to make ten petals, then stretch each one across its width to curve it (see figure 4 on page 76).

To make the flower centre, take a piece of scrap paper and roll it into a small ball. Cover this ball with a piece of black crêpe paper, stretched smoothly round it and its edges twisted together at the base (see figure 6 on page 72). Surround this ball with a fringe of stamens: cut a length of black crêpe paper across the grain, twice as wide as the height of the ball, and cut a fine fringe along one side of it, to half its width. Wrap it round the central ball and secure at the base with fuse wire (2).

Position the petals round the centre and secure their bases with fuse wire wrapped tightly round them and the flower centre (3). Make a stem as for a rose (see figure 7 on page 76) and cover the flower-head base and the stem with green paper.

Finish off by making two sets of sepals (see figure 9 on page 72) from strips of paper about 4 cm ($1\frac{1}{2}$ in) wide and 8 cm (3 in) long. Wrap one of these round the base of the flower-head and the other a little further down the stem, gluing them in place (4).

Leaves

To make leaves, use the templates given here (5–7) or take their shape from nature. You can enlarge or reduce the shapes for larger or smaller flowers.

You will need: green crêpe paper; thick or thin wire, depending on the size of the leaf; PVA glue.

Method

For each leaf, cut two identical shapes in crêpe paper. Cut a length of wire at least 25 mm (1 in) longer than the leaf; its length will depend on the size of the leaf and how it will be attached to the main flower stem. Cover the wire with a strip of crêpe paper (unless the leaf is to be attached to the main stem at its base), then glue it centrally on one leaf shape (see figure 7 on page 72), with one end of the wire forming the stem. Stick the other leaf shape directly on top so that the wire is sandwiched between them and forms the leaf's central vein.

Sometimes several leaflets form one leaf, as in the case of a rose or peony, so they must be bound together on one leaf stem which is then attached to the main flower stem. To do this, make one leaf with a covered wire stem and an even number with bare wire. The leaf with covered wire is the terminal leaflet, the rest are opposite pairs of laterals. Cut a length of wire for the leaf stem and bind the terminal leaflet to one end of it with a green crêpe paper strip. Continue winding the strip down the leaf stem, binding in the laterals in opposite pairs as you do so (8).

Make as many leaves as are needed for one flower and bind them to the main stem with a strip of crêpe paper.

Waxing flowers

You can give paper flowers a realistic sheen by waxing their petals, as shown in the photograph on page 75. This is not as difficult as it sounds, but care must be taken not the splash the hot wax when the flower-heads are dipped, as it is highly inflammable.

You will need: paper flowers; a block of translucent paraffin wax, glycerine; a large old saucepan; a heatproof container large enough to hold a flower-head.

Method
Put as much wax as you think will cover a flower-head into the heatproof container. Place it in a saucepan containing about 12 mm ($\frac{1}{2}$ in) of water, and heat until the wax melts. Remove the pan from the heat and add a few drops of glycerine to the melted wax: this will help stop it cracking when dry.

Hold a flower by the stem and immerse the head in the wax, making sure that all the petals receive a thin coating. Lift out the flower after about five seconds, and keep holding it upside down over the container so that the excess wax drips back into it. Too much wax drying on the flowers will cause blobs to form and spoil the smooth appearance of the petals. Hang them upside down to dry.

Before they dry you can arrange the petals if they have been pushed out of shape during waxing; use a pair of blunt-ended tweezers or other blunt metal instrument. (Do not touch the flowers with the fingers, as the wax will lose its sheen if it is handled.)

Garlands

Short garlands of small and medium-sized flowers can be used to make pretty, summery necklaces and headbands, while longer garlands can be made with larger blooms and worn Hawaiian-style for parties. Several lengths of garlands can be used for decorations on an even grander scale, for example festooned round a tablecloth for a special-occasion buffet (as in the photograph on page 78).

You will need: assorted paper flowers (complete with leaves and stems); adhesive tape, string, wire, strong thread or drawing pins to secure the garland if required.

Method
Garlands for most purposes look better if there is as little stem showing as possible, so use plenty of flowers. Join them together simply by twisting their stems round each other (1). When you have made the length you require, go back over it and fill in any gaps with more flowers and perhaps foliage. Keep the flower-heads close together and bend them so that they face different directions. You could tie in real evergreen foliage with fine wire if you are short of flowers and the garland still needs filling out.

To finish a circular garland, simply wind the stems at either end of the length together, and neaten them with a crêpe paper strip bound round them if desired.

Fabric flowers

Some of the most effective fabric flowers are the simplest kind of all to make, and they look marvellous in sumptuous fabrics such as satins, silks and velvets. You don't have to make them look realistic; indeed, the fun of making these flowers is that they can be purely fanciful. For example, the stylized five-petalled satin blooms which add a touch of glamour to this straw hat are not meant to be true representations of a particular flower; what matters is that the apricot and cream colours complement the plain straw of the hat, lifting it out of the ordinary, and that their shapes are pleasing.

Very few materials are needed: beautiful flowers can be created from scraps of fabric left over from dressmaking and other sewing projects, so it can cost next to nothing to make them. Fabric flowers are especially suitable for hats and clothes in general (see page 89 for how to make a four-flower sprig into an attractive brooch) as they are not easily damaged: if a flower is squashed or bent its wire outline means that it can simply be pushed back into shape.

Tools & materials

Fabric Most fabrics are suitable for flower-making, although fairly stiff materials such as heavyweight linen or glazed cotton are the easiest to use and therefore best for beginners. Limp, delicate fabrics like organdie and crêpe, which are a little more difficult to handle when cutting and sticking, are best used after you have had practice with other fabrics. This is an ideal craft for using remnants of fabric, especially when you are experimenting with designs and techniques, as even the smallest scraps can be used to make a petal. Before making a flower, think of the purpose you intend for it, and match the fabric to its function as well as its form. For example, more expensive fabrics such as silk, satin and velvet are best used for special-occasion flowers such as roses, orchids or lilies to decorate wedding hats or formal dresses, while small, delicate broderie anglaise blooms would suit a posy for a guest room, and bright gingham 'daisies' would be appropriate in a kitchen arrangement.

Wire Fine thread-covered wire, available in various colours from hobby shops, is needed to construct each petal shape. It is usually available in 9 m (10 yd) reels, so that even if you only buy one or two reels you will be able to make a huge number of flowers. You can also use milliner's wire, obtainable from haberdashers, which is very similar. Both types of wire bend easily to form all sorts of shapes. Fine, coloured florist's wire can also be used for petals, but is less easily obtainable. For stems, use plain florist's stub wire, the kind used for fresh flowers (see page 8), or galvanized reel wire.

Stamens These are available ready-made from hobby shops in packets of different colours, some with 'pearl' or beaded tips which make very attractive flower-centres for silk or satin flowers used as jewellery. Alternatively, you can make stamens from lengths of twisted fine wire.

Florist's tape (gutta-percha) This self-adhesive tape, also used for fresh flowers (see page 8), is required in the making of fabric flowers to wind round the base of a flower-head to hold the petals together, and to cover the wire stems of the flowers by being bound round them.

Wire cutters Either these or a small pair of pliers, though not essential (scissors may be used to cut fine wire), are nevertheless useful for positioning and bending wire into petal and bud shapes, as well as cutting it.

Adhesive Use a latex adhesive such as Copydex, which does not leave marks, to stick fabric to wire, or a clear general-purpose glue that dries quickly, such as Uhu.

Scissors Sharp scissors are essential for cutting fabric. If you are using scissors to cut wire, keep an old pair just for this purpose, as it makes them blunt.

Leaves You can of course make your own leaf from pieces of fabric (see page 88), but ready-made leaves of stiffened paper (from craft shops) make convincing additions to the stems of fabric flowers.

Felt-tip pens A range of these pens in different colours is useful for putting markings on petals, if desired.

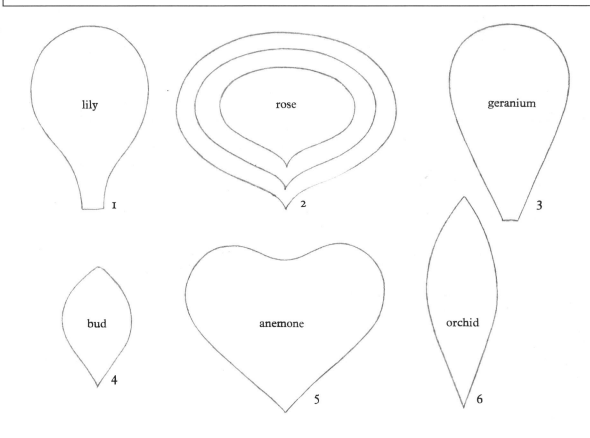

lily 1

rose 2

geranium 3

bud 4

anemone 5

orchid 6

Making fabric flowers

All the flowers described in this chapter are made by the same basic method, whereby each petal is formed by bending fine thread-covered wire to the desired shape and sticking it to fabric which is then cut round it. You can make all sorts of petal shapes – the wire is very flexible – and it is a good idea to experiment by making a few different shapes before assembling a flower. Six drawings of suggested petal shapes are given here (1–6), but many more are possible. These petals – named for convenience – are not intended to be lifelike copies of real flower petals, although you can make more realistic-looking flowers such as pansies and primulas, using the same basic method. Use the drawings as templates or enlarge or reduce them as required, depending on the type of flower being made, or work from your own templates. Make as few as four petals for a simple flower, or fifteen or more of graduated size for a full-blown rose.

You will need: pieces of fabric; reels of thread-covered wire in various colours; florist's stub wire or galvanized wire; florist's tape; stamens; wire cutters; sharp scissors, adhesive.

Method

To make each petal, first take a length of thread-covered wire and bend it to the desired petal shape (using a template as a guide if necessary). Lay your chosen fabric flat, right side up, then apply glue lightly to one side of the wire shape and stick it to the fabric, pressing it down firmly all round to ensure that it sticks to the fabric. When the glue is dry, cut round the outside of the wire as closely as possible to the edge (7): the glue will stop the fabric from fraying. Pull away any rubbery bits of glue that remain attached. Make as many petals as required in this way, choosing wire either to match or contrast with the fabric.

To complete the flower, take a suitable length of florist's wire for the stem and make a small hook at one end of it, bending it round with pliers if necessary. Take a bunch of stamens and bend them all in half, loop them firmly round the stem hook (8) and squeeze tightly. Holding this centre in one hand, position the petals round it (right sides facing inward) so that they are standing quite upright like a closed flower-head. For positioning buds, see instructions below. Now take a short length of fine wire, say about 10 cm (4 in), and wind it tightly round the ends of the petals, enclosing the stamens and joining the petals to the stem (9). Finally, wrap florist's tape round the base of the flower-head and along the stem (10), then bend out the petals (11).

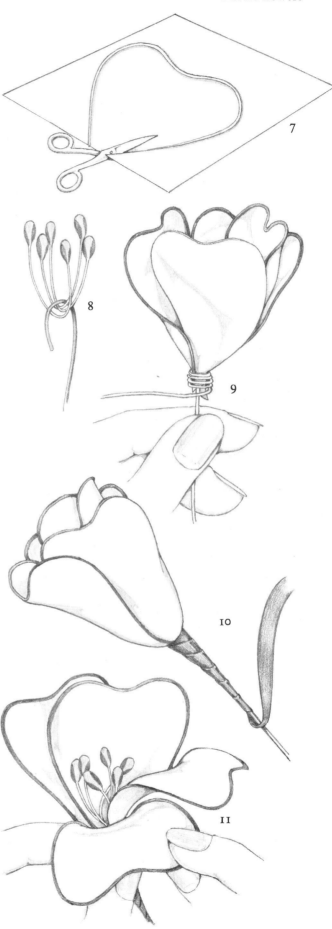

See page 89 for details of how to make a four-flower sprig like this stylish cream and fuschia brooch (above), which adds a touch of vivid colour to a simple black dress. Note how the colour of the wire has been chosen to contrast with the colour of the petals.

Silk and satin flowers in shades of cream, pale pink, apricot and rose pink (right) make an elegant arrangement which will delight a special guest. To make the full-blown roses, you need twelve petals of varying sizes (see page 84, figure 2, for the templates).
Make three small bud-shaped petals for the centre, then four larger ones with wide tops narrowing to their base for the middle ring of petals, then five even larger ones for the outer layer. Make sure that the central petals are securely joined to the rest of the flower-head at its base. The other flowers shown here have two, four or five petals, and some have inner buds, both wired and unwired. The effect of the flowers can be varied by using contrasting wire, as here, even though only two or three colours are used for the entire arrangement, and also by wrapping two or more flower stems together to make a sprig. For the basic method of making the flowers, see pages 84–5.

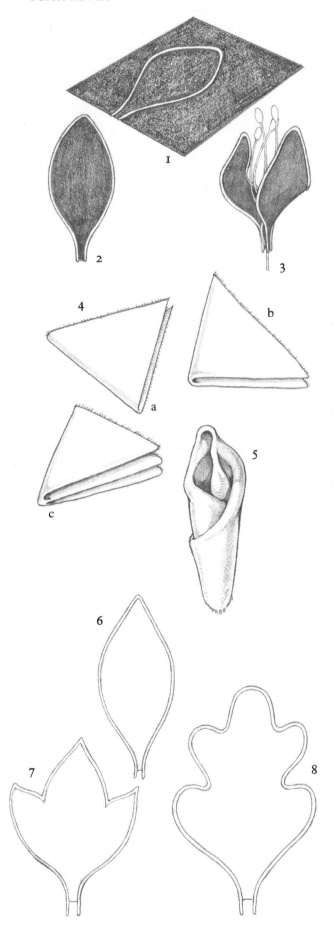

To make buds, either large ones to stand alone or with others on one stem (such as the one in the brooch shown on page 86), or for a centre to a five-petalled flower (see the example on page 87), use exactly the same technique as for petal making, but in this case make two shapes only (see figure 4, page 84) and position them so that their right side – the wired side – faces outwards (**1**). This is so that after the parts of the bud have been assembled (**2** and **3**) the right side of the fabric will be showing, since they will remain in their upright position in order to look like newly unfurling petals.

To make an unwired pointed bud like the one in the centre of the two-petalled satin lily shown on page 87, take a square piece of soft fabric in a colour to complement the petals, and fold it in half to make a triangle. Then fold it again into another triangle, and fold it a third time in the same way (**4**). Fold back the corners of the raw edge so that they overlap (**5**), and secure with a blob of glue or length of fuse wire wrapped tightly round it. This is the base of the bud. Make up the flower as already described (page 85), pushing the hook of the stem through the layers of fabric at this point, before attaching the petals round this central bud by means of fine wire and florist's tape.

To make leaves, either buy ready-made leaves of stiffened paper (patterned to look like fabric), or use green fabric of a suitable weight to match the flower, and thread-covered wire (of perhaps a darker or lighter green for contrast), and make them in the same way as petals. The only difference is that the wire, having been bent into the leaf shape, should not be cut off close to the fabric: the ends should be allowed to extend beyond it so that they can be wrapped round the stem or flower base as required.

Use the patterns given for three different leaf shapes (**6–8**) if you wish. The leaves themselves can be arranged on the stem in different ways: singly, as opposite pairs, or as alternate leaves. If the leaf stem is to be quite long, cover it with a piece of florist's tape, but leave enough wire at the ends to wrap round the main stem, to be bound in with the tape coming from the flower-head (see page 85).

Using fabric flowers

By following the basic techniques described in this chapter and adapting the petal shapes given on page 84, you will be able to make many kinds of flower for different decorative purposes. The simplest flowers – lilies – have only two petals and a soft inner bud or stamens (**1**), but look just as effective as those made up of four or five petals and a decorative centre – such as the anemone (**2**) and the geranium (**3**). Any one of these may be all that is needed to give a focal point to a plain garment, whereas more complex blooms composed of layers of petals – like the rose (**4**) – may look best in arrangements like the one shown on page 87.

Large versions of all these flowers can be used individually to decorate many items around the home, and would look splendid sewn on to the hem of plain curtains or a bedspread, or along the edges of a tablecloth for a special-occasion buffet. Smaller flowers are better suited to more delicate items such as a brooch (see below) or hair ornament.

To decorate a hat

It is important to give careful thought to the effect you want to achieve, and to the sort of flower and fabric most suitable for the type of hat you wish to decorate. For example, a single silk orchid (**5**) could look marvellous on a summer hat for a wedding or garden party, while a bunch of felt anemones or pansies would be most appropriate on a winter cloche for everyday wear. A straw hat can be given a fresh, summery look with a circle of white cotton daisies round the band, while a more formal effect could be achieved with just two satin orchids attached to the brim, as in the photograph on page 82.

Make the flowers, leaves and buds according to the basic methods described on pages 85 and 88, using shorter stem wires than you would for a vase arrangement, and arrange them on the hat to your satisfaction. If the hat has a ribbon round it, you may be able to attach the flowers to this with safety pins, disguising the pins if necessary with a bud or foliage. You may wish to make the decoration permanent: if so, sew the flowers to the hat.

To make a brooch

To make a four-flowered sprig brooch like the one shown on page 86, choose flower shapes which go well together and will be suitable for the elongated shape of the sprig. The brooch shown here comprises one simple geranium shape with a stamen centre at the base, two lilies with unwired inner buds, and a wired bud with stamens at the top (**6**). The method of making them is the same as for the other flowers illustrated in this chapter (see page 85), except that they are on a much smaller scale and so a little more fiddly to make. When each of the flowers is complete with its stem, arrange them in your hand and wrap more florist's tape round all four stems, starting at the point where the stems come together, and taking in a metal brooch fitting (**7**) as you continue wrapping the tape right to the ends of the stems.

Embroidered flowers

Even with the most basic needlework skills, it is possible to sew many beautiful floral decorations surprisingly quickly. The simple embroidery stitches used in this chapter will be familiar to many people, but to help jog rusty memories, or for absolute beginners, there are how-to-sew sketches and descriptions of other relevant techniques overleaf, together with hints on tools and equipment. By referring to these and following the step-by-step instructions for the projects, you will be able to add a personal touch to all sorts of items, like the baby's dress and pillowcase shown on the left, and to make the charming sampler on page 94.

More unusual types of embroidery such as appliqué work and beading, often found on expensive items with exclusive design labels, are here presented in easy-sew methods so that, with commonly available materials and a little imagination, original articles can be created in just a few hours. And home-dressmakers with a sewing machine will be surprised how many 'hand-made' designs can be run up in an evening. It will obviously be simpler to follow the patterns exactly at first, but after a few successes you will discover how easy it is to produce your own designs.

Basic stitches

All instructions are given for right-handed sewers. If you are left-handed, simply reverse the way of working.

Back stitch For lines and outlines. Working from right to left, bring the needle through from the back a stitch length along the design line, and make a stitch backwards, then bring the needle out at the front, a stitch length ahead of the one just made. Insert the needle at the end of the previous stitch, bringing it through to the front the same stitch distance ahead again. Continue to the end of the line.

Stem stitch For lines and outlines. Working from the bottom to the top of a line, bring the needle from the back and make a slanting stitch, then bring the needle through again halfway along this stitch. Keeping the thread on the same side of the stitch line throughout, repeat the steps, always bringing the needle through halfway along the previous stitch.

Chain stitch For lines or infilling. Work from top to bottom. Bring the needle through to the right side of the fabric. Reinsert the needle in the same place and make a stitch, looping the thread under the needle. Insert the needle back into the previous stitch and bring it out, again looping the thread. Repeat for a continuous chain stitch.

Lazy daisy A single chain stitch anchored with a short stitch, this is particularly useful for forming flower petals.

Satin stitch For infilling flower or leaf shapes. Bring the thread through to the left of the design and insert the needle directly opposite, bringing it back on the left immediately beside the first thread. Continue working evenly so that the stitches touch each other and the edges are smooth.

Long and short stitch For filling in large areas and for shading. Make one long then one short stitch, working as for satin stitch, and continue along the row so that the outer edge is smooth but the inner edge is staggered. Work the next row of stitches all the same length but fitting close up to the first line so that the bottom edge of the line remains staggered. Continue in this way until the last row which should usually be worked like the first, with a smooth outer edge.

French knot For centres or fillings. Bring the needle and thread through to the front and hold the thread down with the left thumb. Take the needle over the top of the thread and twist it round the thread twice. Insert the needle as near as possible to

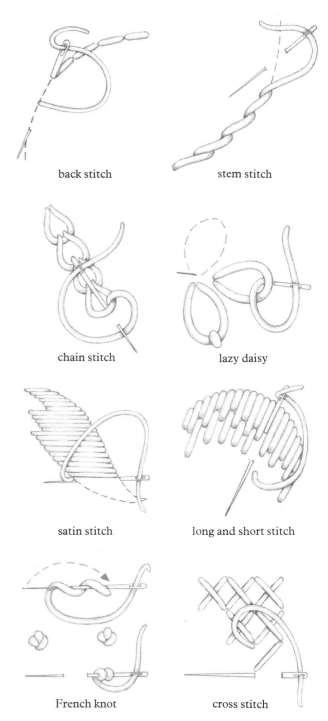

back stitch   stem stitch

chain stitch   lazy daisy

satin stitch   long and short stitch

French knot   cross stitch

where the thread emerges, drawing the thread tightly through the twisted part to form a surface knot.

Cross stitch For lines, outlines and infilling. Working from left to right, make a line of slanting parallel stitches from the lower left line of the cross to the top right, till the line is complete, then finish the crosses by coming back along the line, working from right to left in the same way. (Alternatively, finish both stitches of each cross before going on to the next.)

Tools & materials

Needles Different types are needed for different sewing methods, their size depending on the weight of fabric and thread being used. A bodkin or darning needle is a large, blunt needle with a large eye, used for threading string, wool, ribbon and thonging. Beading needles are long, fine and sharp, with a small eye. Crewel needles, used for most hand embroidery, are long and sharp with a slim eye, and available in packets of assorted sizes.

Ring frame This is not essential, but useful for keeping embroidery fabric or canvas taut when it is being worked. Two wooden rings fit one inside the other with a screw on the outer ring for adjusting tension, and are available in a number of sizes. To use, lay the material smoothly over the smaller ring with the design to be embroidered central, then fit the outer ring over the fabric, push it down over the smaller ring, and tighten the tension screw.

Scissors Small, sharp scissors are needed for general work, including cutting threads. Dressmaker's shears – very sharp with handles curved away from the cutting blade to ensure smooth passage through material – should only be used to cut fabric. For cutting paper, which quickly makes scissors blunt, keep an old pair just for this purpose.

Sewing machine A straight-stitch machine, as the name implies, can only do straight stitching for seams and basic sewing, while a swing-needle machine can also do zigzag, satin stitch and other embroidery stitches, according to the setting of the stitch-width regulator.

Threads Stranded cotton is the most widely used embroidery thread. It is made up of six strands, but can be sub-divided into thicknesses of two or three strands if a finer effect is required. A colour may be lighter than it looks on the skein when worked with only a few threads. Tapestry wool is a 4-ply yarn used mainly on canvas, and also for decorative work such as on knitted clothes.

Transferring designs

Tracing paper or greaseproof paper Used for copying designs. Place the paper over the design and anchor in place, then draw along the outlines with a soft pencil.

Dressmaker's carbon paper Used to transfer the traced design to the fabric (but not suitable for rough-textured material). It is available in packets of different colours; choose a shade which will show up on the fabric and place it, shiny side down, between the fabric and the tracing. Trace over the design so that the outlines are transferred to the fabric (1).

To enlarge or reduce the size of the design you wish to transfer, use the graph pattern, or grid, method. Many designs in crafts books will already be on a grid, but you can make one simply by drawing a rectangle round your design and dividing it into equal squares. Take a sheet of paper and draw the rectangle again with the same number of squares, but proportionately larger or smaller than the first one according to the size of design required. Alternatively, use graph paper or dressmaker's pattern paper which already have a grid pattern printed on them. Then, square by square, carefully copy the lines of the design on to the larger or smaller grid (2).

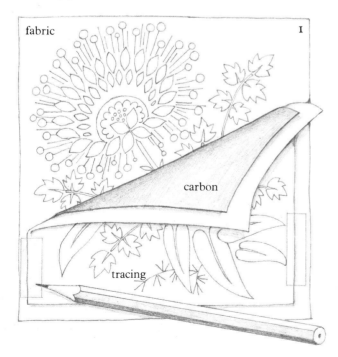

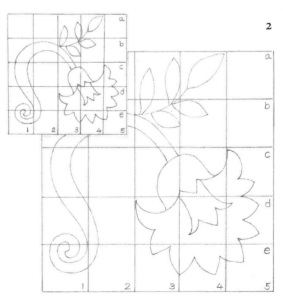

Sampler

This sampler, created to commemorate the birth of a baby, has been designed for evenly woven linen or canvas and is worked by counting the threads of the weave. The design measures 205 mm × 152 mm (8 in × 6 in), with each segment of the border measuring about 17 mm ($\frac{11}{16}$ in) wide, and each stitch (except those for the lettering, the flowers and the cradle) going over three threads of the canvas. The design can, however, be reduced or enlarged by embroidering over two or four threads. You can take the finished sampler to a gallery for framing, or, as here, find an attractive old frame and work a sampler to fit it.

You will need: evenly woven linen or canvas at least 30 cm × 25 cm (12 in × 10 in); stranded embroidery cottons such as Anchor in ten colours – blue, violet, dark green, light green, bright pink, light brown, dark brown, red, salmon pink and yellow; a crewel needle; a ring frame; tracing and carbon paper; a glazed picture frame to fit the sampler, and latex glue, tacks, mounting card and plywood or hardboard for the backing.

Method
Each square of the grid pattern overleaf represents the number of canvas threads you want in each stitch. For a larger or smaller sampler, practise sewing over more or fewer threads with one section of the border pattern on a spare corner of the canvas.

one section
of border pattern

JAMES

MOTHER   FATHER

Put the canvas in a ring frame (see page 93). Take lengths of blue embroidery cotton for the border and divide the lengths in two so that each one consists of three strands. Working in back stitch and leaving enough cotton at the start of the stitching to fasten off at the back of the work, sew all round the border, always embroidering over and under the same number of threads of the canvas. Finish off by sewing into the back of the stitches.

Following the design, work the tree in cross stitch, continuing to embroider over the same number of threads with each stitch. Work the trunk first (dark green), then work one side of the pattern completely before going on to the other, using light green for the branches and adding pink flowers at the ends of the leaves.

Now cross-stitch the two hexagonal shapes and the border round the cradle. For the words Mother and Father, transfer them from the pattern to the linen (see page 93) and work them in satin stitch.

Work out your own lettering for the baby's name, either by tracing out the letters required from a newspaper or by obtaining a book of printed alphabets from a library. Draw up the name on a sheet of graph paper, clearly marking diagonal, horizontal and vertical lines. When transferring the name to the canvas, you can work over a different number of threads at a time, depending on the length of the name and its size. Use back stitch.

Transfer the outline of the cradle from the pattern to the sampler. Work the basket in back stitch, using two shades of brown, the lighter colour for the vertical stitches (work two side by side) and the darker for the horizontal (work three side by side). Use stem stitch to outline the front of the cradle hood, long and short stitch for the cover, in violet.

Transfer the flowers for the lower corners to the canvas, and use long and short stitch for the petals (red and salmon), French knots for the centres (yellow).

Remove the sampler from the frame and lightly press on the wrong side with a medium iron, using a cloth between the back of the embroidery and the iron.

Before framing the sampler you must back it to ensure that it remains stretched. Take a piece of stiff mounting card of the same size as the internal dimensions of the frame, and position the sampler centrally on it. Leaving a wide enough margin round the design to give a good turnover to the back of the card, cut off any excess canvas and pull the edges round to the back of the card, making diagonal cuts at the corners so that they will lie flat. Use dabs of glue to stick down the edges of the canvas.

Fit the sampler into the glazed frame, add another sheet of mounting card the same size as the canvas to prevent the sampler rubbing against the backing board (which might discolour it over a long period) and back with hardboard or plywood, fixed to the frame with headless tacks (brads). Use a bradawl to make holes for the tacks if necessary.

Baby's dress & pillowcase

This simple cross-stitch design in bright, cheerful colours adds interest to a baby's plain white dress and matching pillowcase (photograph on pages 90–1).

You will need: a crewel needle; three different coloured skeins of a light-weight thread such as Anchor stranded cotton (which can be separated so that it is not too thick for the fine fabric of the dress); paper; a pencil; tracing paper; scissors; adhesive tape such as Sellotape; dressmaker's carbon paper.

Method
Trace off the design (1) as described on page 93, folding the tracing paper in half so that the folded edge lies along the centre line of the pattern. (Add extra motifs for a larger dress.) Open out the paper and trace again to complete the design.

Now cut round the tracing to within 4 mm ($\frac{1}{8}$ in) of the design. Cut a piece of dressmaker's carbon paper slightly larger than the pattern, choosing a colour that shows up on the fabric but will not clash with the stitches. Sandwich the carbon paper, shiny side down, between the fabric and the pattern, securing both sheets of paper to the material with clear adhesive tape which will not make marks and is easily removed. (Do not use pins as they will cause the fabric to pucker.)

With the needle, prick through the corners of every square of the pattern, carefully lifting the carbon after several squares have been completed to make sure that the action is hard enough to transfer the carbon colour to the material (2). When all the pattern has been successfully copied, remove both tracing and carbon paper.

Cut the stranded cotton into easily managed lengths, say about 40 cm (16 in), so that it does not become tangled in use. Divide each length into three so that the cotton is only two strands thick. For a thicker fabric increase the number of strands in each length.

Begin cross-stitching the design, working with one colour at a time so that you complete all parts of the pattern in that shade before moving on to another. Take the cotton from the wrong side of the material through to the right side, leaving 5 cm (2 in) to sew into the back of the finished stitches. This method of finishing off is better than knots which frequently come undone and feel knobbly under delicate fabrics.

Following the first cross-stitch method (page 92) work half the stitch of the motif, a line at a time, finishing the stitch on the way back. Do this with all three colours until the design is complete.

As a final touch, to pinpoint the flower design, French knots can be worked in a suitable shade at intervals along, say, the dress hem or added to smocking as here. Use the same method and design to embroider the matching pillowcase.

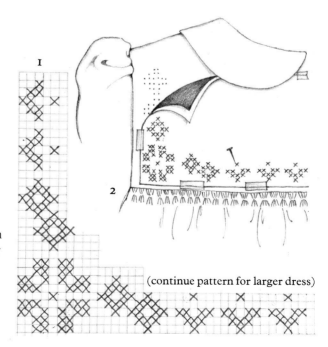

(continue pattern for larger dress)

Beaded evening bag

The design to be beaded is for a bag measuring 20 cm (8 in) across. The instructions are for a black bag, but you could use a bag and beads of different colours just as effectively.

You will need: a plain black evening bag with a flap front; five boxes of differently coloured small, round glass beads (red, orange, white, blue and green) for the poppy and its leaves; fifty single long oval gold beads (for the wheat ears); a beading needle; tracing paper; carbon paper; adhesive tape; a hard lead pencil; black cotton thread.

Method
Unpick the lining from the front flap of the evening bag, taking care not to let either the lining or the material fray. Pin the lining out of the way by securing it inside the bag.

Transfer the design to tracing paper from the grid pattern on page 100, enlarging or reducing it if the size of your bag differs from that of the one shown here. Cut out the pattern, trimming the paper close to the edges of the design, as described for the baby's cross-stitch dress (page 97).

Place a sheet of suitably coloured dressmaker's carbon paper (yellow will show up well on a black background) between the bag front and the pattern. Fix both pieces of paper in position on the front of the bag and attach with adhesive tape. Draw along all the lines of the design with a pencil to impress the pattern on to the fabric.

Begin the beading at the outer edges of the design, working inwards and completing each outlined section before going on to the next (**1**). Using cotton that matches the colour of the bag, secure a length with a knot at the back of the design on the edge of the first petal. Bring the needle through to the right side of the material. Thread four to six beads of the first colour (here, red), at a time, then take the needle back to the wrong side of the material. Make

Beading is an exciting way of enlivening many plain articles, particularly for glamorous occasions. The poppy design on this evening bag (above) is made using small round glass beads for the flower and its leaves, and larger oval gold beads for the wheat ears. As the bag is a relatively firm object and the design is bold, the beading can be done using the simple method of threading several beads on to one stitch. For beading work on finer or softer fabrics, or for more intricate patterns, it would probably be better to stitch each bead individually.

Off-the-peg woollens such as cardigans and sweaters can be given an exclusive look with the addition of a little hand embroidery. This cardigan (right) is worked in soft shades of green, rose, coral, salmon, blue, aubergine, grape, bronze and ochre. These subtle colours give a mellow effect against the pale grey background of the cardigan, but more striking colours could be used to enhance a brighter background. Instructions on page 100.

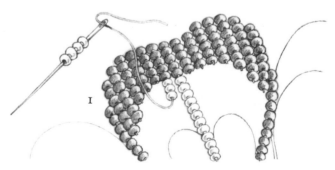

I

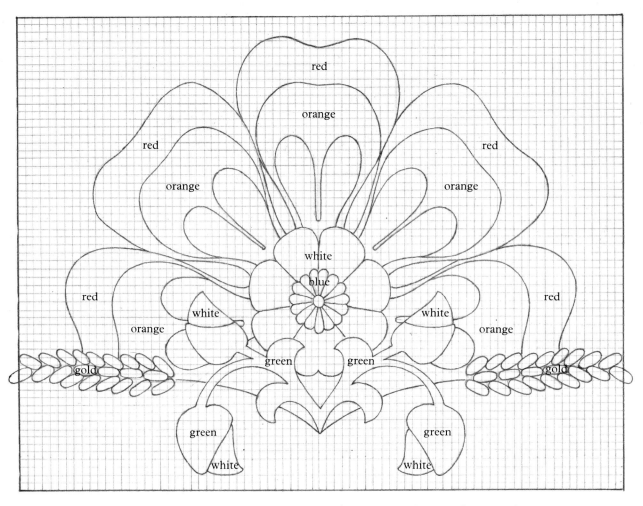

a small stitch to secure and bring the needle through to the right side again.

With the second and subsequent stitches thread one or two beads more or less than previously, depending on the shape of the outline, to achieve the curving shapes of the petals. Continue infilling all the outer sections of the petals in this way, using the same colour, until they are complete.

Fill in the middle area of the petals with the next colour beads (orange) in exactly the same way, this time altering the number of beads to as few as two or three when shaping the sides and inner sections. When all five petals are beaded, use the same method to fill in the poppy centre, the buds and the leaves with blue, white, and green beads.

Finally, stitch each one of the long oval beads in place one at a time in the shape of the two wheat ears. It is easiest to begin at the tip of each ear and work round the outer edges before filling in the central row.

When all the beading is complete, resew the lining into the bag front to cover up the wrong side of the design.

Embroidered cardigan

Only five stitches – long and short stitch, satin stitch, stem stitch, lazy daisy and French knots – are used to make this pretty floral design, which is worked in tapestry wool. The pattern is transferred to loosely woven muslin which is tacked in place on to the cardigan. The embroidery is worked over the muslin which is then pulled out from under it, a few strands at a time. Tapestry wool lends itself well to this type of freehand sewing on wool if the skeins are divided in two to give a smoother finish on the finely knitted fabric.

You will need: a plain cardigan or sweater; eleven different coloured skeins of tapestry wool such as Anchor; crewel needle; tracing paper; squared pattern paper (if the design is to be enlarged or reduced); dressmaker's carbon paper; ball-point pen; piece of muslin a little larger than the pattern; small scissors; tacking thread; tweezers.

Method
Using the method described on page 93, transfer the design from the pattern (1) with a ball-point pen

on to a piece of loose-weave muslin. Pin the muslin pattern firmly in place on the cardigan and secure it with tacking stitches.

Work one colour at a time with easily manageable lengths of wool, each length divided in two. The key below describes where to use each stitch. As the chains forming the lazy daisy flowers give them a more open look than the dense satin stitch ones, fill them in with a small running stitch from the centre to the top of each petal. It is not necessary to work the stitches in any particular order, apart from the

French knots which should be done last; then you can work as many French knots as are needed to fill in the flower centres.

When the embroidery is completed, trim the muslin to within 4 mm ($\frac{1}{8}$ in) of the design. Take a pair of tweezers and gently pull the strands of muslin out from under the embroidery (2). The muslin will come away quite easily so long as it is pulled carefully, a few strands at a time. The same design can then be worked in reverse on the other side of the cardigan in exactly the same way.

Key

1 pale green
2 mid green
3 rose
4 coral
5 salmon
6 light blue
7 navy blue
8 aubergine
9 grape
10 bronze
11 ochre

The large petals and leaves are worked in satin stitch and long and short stitch, the small petals in lazy daisy, the buds and flower centres in French knots, and the stems in stem stitch.

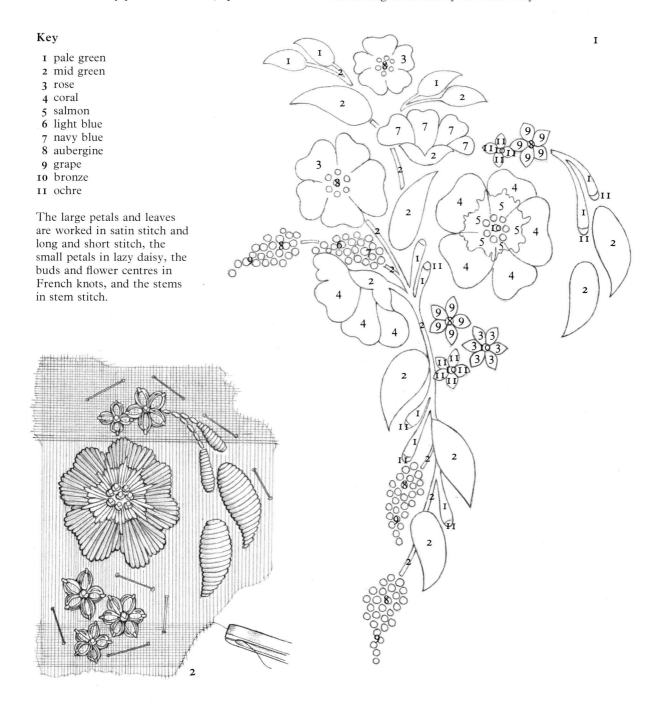

Appliqué

Machine-sewn appliqué works looks just as spectacular as the hand-sewn variety and takes only a fraction of the time. This pretty tablecloth (instructions on pages 104–5) was created from a piece of sheeting and a remnant of floral curtain material, although a plain cotton cloth and pieces of dress fabric in complementary colours would look just as effective. Sheeting is useful for making tablecloths as it is wide enough for most tables without having to be joined with a seam. Make sure all colours are fast and that you do not use materials of different fibres for the same cloth if they cannot be washed together.

For machine-sewn appliqué on fabrics that fray you will need a swing-needle (zigzag) sewing machine that does satin stitch. This should present no problem on a fully automatic machine, but you may need to experiment with the closeness of the zigzag stitches on a semi-automatic or to use buttonhole stitch. If you have a straight-stitch machine you may be able to buy a zigzag attachment.

Not only the appliquéd pieces of fabric but also the scalloped edges of the cloth (detail below) are sewn with satin stitch. This method is simpler than hemming and also neater, as it avoids the bulk of layers of folded material.

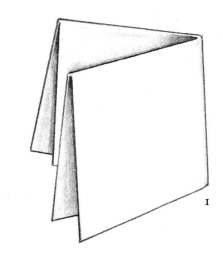

I

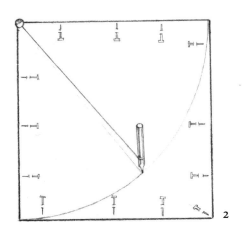

2

3

Appliquéd tablecloth

For a circular tablecloth, calculate the amount of fabric needed by measuring the diameter of the table and adding twice the desired overhang. Allow enough fabric to cut a square with sides equal to this total measurement. No hem allowance is required.

For a rectangular or square tablecloth, measure the length and width of the table instead of the diameter, and draw the scallops (see figure 4) along the straight edges of the cloth. No hem allowance is required.

You will need: a piece of sheeting fabric cut to the measurements described above; offcuts of floral curtain fabric to make the appliqué flowers; sewing thread to match the colours of your fabric; dressmaker's pins; drawing pin; length of string or binding tape; pencil; piece of card or stiff paper for scallop template; cup or similar curved shape; large and small scissors.

Method

Fold the sheeting fabric in half, then in half again, as shown (**1**). Pin along the folds to avoid any movement of the cloth. To cut out a circle, put a drawing pin into the central corner of the fabric and attach it to a flat surface such as the floor or a piece of hardboard on the work surface, laying the fabric flat. Cut a piece of string or binding tape the length of one of the folded edges, plus enough to be anchored by the drawing pin at one end and tied round a pencil at the other. Attach it in this way and draw an arc round the folded cloth (**2**). Cut along this pencil line through all four layers of fabric. Unfold the cloth which now forms a complete circle.

To form the scalloped edge, first make a template. Take a straight-sided piece of card, say about 75 mm (3 in) wide and, using a cup or similar curved shape, draw a quarter circle across it, making sure that there is about 12 mm ($\frac{1}{2}$ in) of card between the base of the curve and the straight edge (**3**). This forms the template. Cut it out and mark a line 6 mm ($\frac{1}{4}$ in) from and parallel to the straight edge of the card. When the template is positioned on the cloth, the edge of the fabric must always be on this line, to ensure that the scallops are all the same distance from the edge.

Position the template on the right side of the cloth and draw round it with a pencil (**4**), continuing until the cloth is scalloped all the way round. If, when you finish drawing the scallops, there is only room for part of one to complete the circle, you can position your appliqué over it to hide it. Do not cut round the scallops at this stage.

Now cut out the flowers and leaves for the appliqué work, trimming them close to the edge of the various shapes with small scissors. Place them round the edge of the cloth as required and arrange each group until a harmonious effect is achieved. Tack them securely in place (5).

Using small satin stitches, sew one colour at a time. At the start and finish of a colour, leave enough thread at the back to fasten off by hand-sewing a running stitch into the back of the satin stitches. Do not machine too fast in case the material puckers. When all the appliqué work is complete tidy up the loose ends and snip them off.

Now machine-stitch along the pencilled scalloped shapes, again using small satin stitches and using thread of a colour that either complements the main shade of the cloth or provides a striking contrast, and finish off as before.

Finally, cut round all the scallops as closely as possible to the satin stitch and following the outline of any appliqué flowers or leaves that project beyond them (6).

Matching napkins can easily be made in the same way as the cloth from left-over pieces of fabric.

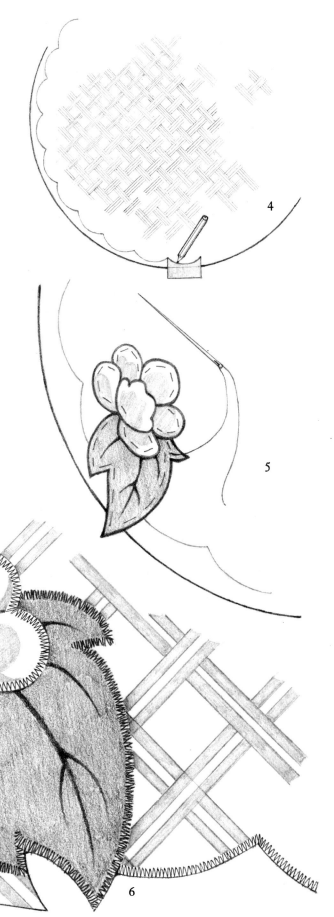

Poppy cushion

Appliqué work with leather is an interesting way of using the cheaper offcuts of leather you can buy, and can be done with a straight-stitch machine as the material does not fray. This cheerful cushion cover with poppy motif is easily sewn with soft leather on most machines, but consult the instruction book for your model first and practise on a few scraps to find the correct stitch length and tension. A medium needle (90/14) with a medium stitch length (no. 3) and normal tension should work very well.

Several of the appliqué pieces are glued into position before being sewed. Glue lightly but with a strong natural latex adhesive, gluing one section at a time and making sure that the piece does not move out of position. The stems are given a quilted effect: muslin is sewn to the back of these parts of the pattern and stuffed with dishcloth cotton or wool, which raises the surface of the leather above the rest of the design.

You will need: offcuts of soft leather – the type used to make gloves is best – in black, red, green and dark red; graph pattern paper; pencil; 25 cm (10 in) muslin; latex adhesive such as Copydex; a large bodkin; small ball of wool, or dishcloth cotton; thread to match the leather; a cushion pad 46 cm (18 in) square; black velvet, satin or cotton 50 cm (20 in) square for the cushion back.

Method
First use a cool iron on the wrong side of the leather to take out any creases. Then enlarge the design (page 109), to 46 cm (18 in) square, using the graph paper method described on page 93, and cut out all the pattern pieces.

With right sides together, using black thread, machine black leather piece 2 to piece 3 with a straight seam. Continue joining all the black pieces in turn (3 to 4, 4 to 5 etc.) until piece 8 is joined. Join this piece to piece 1, leaving pieces 1 and 2 unjoined. Press all the seams open with a cool iron.

Lay these joined pieces right side up on a flat surface with pieces 1 and 2 edge to edge. Mark out the position of the flower bud and stem as shown on the pattern plan.

To make the bud, place the green leather bud shape right side down on a work surface and position the smaller red centre, also face down, over the cut-out centre, exactly in the middle so that there is an equal seam allowance all round. Lightly glue the edges of the red centre to the green bud shape (1).

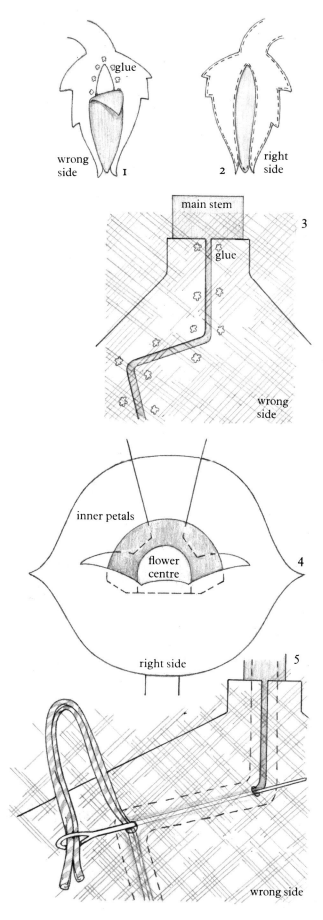

wrong side **1**

2 right side

main stem

3

glue

wrong side

inner petals

flower centre

4

right side

5

wrong side

When the glue is dry, the centre of the bud can be stitched in place. Thread the machine with green thread and, with right side uppermost, sew 2 mm ($\frac{1}{16}$ in) in from the inner edge (**2**).

Position the flower bud and stem (parts 1 and 2) on the cushion as shown on the pattern plan, and glue in position ready for stitching. Do the same with the main stem, gluing it in position centrally over the open edges of the black leather.

Turn to the wrong side of the leather and position a piece of muslin 30 cm (12 in) by 18 cm (7 in) over both stems and glue in place (**3**). Turn the leather to the right side and stitch all round the stems 2 mm ($\frac{1}{16}$ in) in from the edges, through the layers of leather and muslin, to make channels for the stuffing.

To make the flower, glue the seam allowances of the flower centre (the black and green shapes) under the dark red petal shape as shown, and the dark red seam allowances under the black (**4**). Then lightly glue the dark red petal shape on to the lighter red petal shape.

Glue the assembled flower in position on the black leather. Using dark red cotton, sew round the dark red petal shape the usual 2 mm ($\frac{1}{16}$ in) from the edge. With light red cotton sew round the light red edges, then use green and black cotton for the centre. Take all threads through to the back, knot and cut.

Turn to the back of the cushion. Thread a large bodkin with a few strands of wool or dishcloth cotton, and insert between the muslin and the leather on the main stem. Push it all the way up the stem, taking the needle out through the muslin at intervals to keep the wool tight, then inserting it back in the same hole so that the stem shape remains smooth. Repeat as many times as necessary to fill the stem sufficiently to push up the green leather on the right side of the cushion (**5**). Do the same with the two sections of the bud stem so that they also stand out.

With right sides facing, pin and tack the fabric for the back to the leather. Machine on three sides and 3 cm (1$\frac{1}{2}$ in) in at either end of the fourth side. Remove the tacking and flatten the open seams with a thumb nail.

Turn the cover right side out and insert the cushion. Turn in the seam on the final side and sew the edges together. Finally, spray the top surface of the cushion with a leather protector to make it dirt repellent.

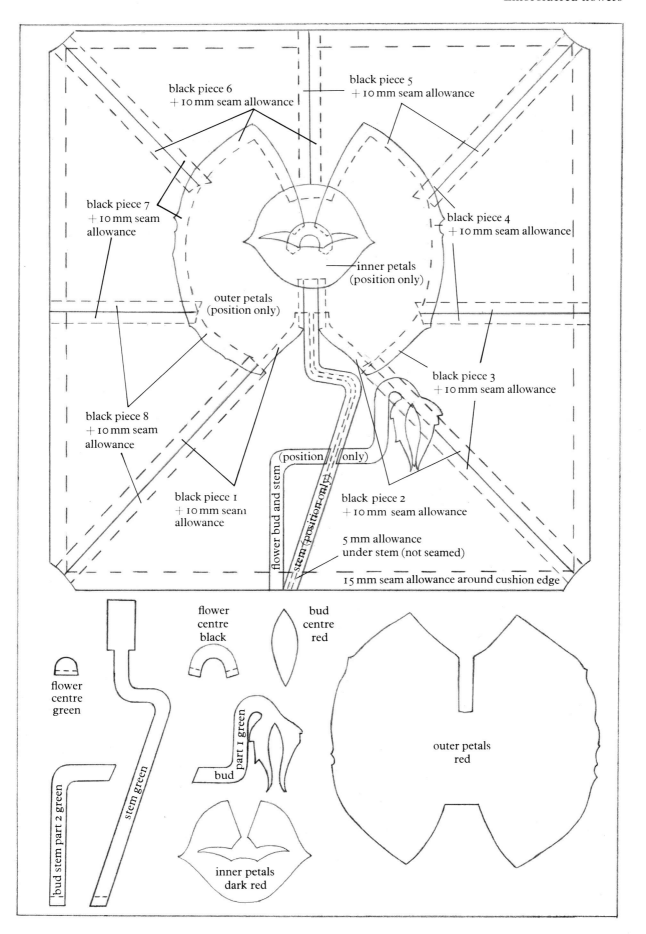

black piece 6
+ 10 mm seam allowance

black piece 5
+ 10 mm seam allowance

black piece 7
+ 10 mm seam
allowance

black piece 4
+ 10 mm seam allowance

inner petals
(position only)

outer petals
(position only)

black piece 3
+ 10 mm seam allowance

black piece 8
+ 10 mm seam
allowance

(position   only)

flower bud and stem

stem (position only)

black piece 1
+ 10 mm seam
allowance

black piece 2
+ 10 mm seam allowance

5 mm allowance
under stem (not seamed)

15 mm seam allowance around cushion edge

flower
centre
black

bud
centre
red

flower
centre
green

bud stem part 2 green

stem green

part 1 green

bud

outer petals
red

inner petals
dark red

Further reading

Bauzen, P. and S. *Flower Pressing* (Oak Tree Press, London 1972)

Condon, G. *Complete Book of Flower Preservation* (Robert Hale, London 1974)

Cullum, E. *A Cottage Herbal* (David & Charles, Newton Abbot 1975)

De Denne, L. *Creative Needlecraft* (Sundial Publications Ltd., London 1979)

Derbyshire, J. and Burgess, R. *Dried and Pressed Flowers* (Hamlyn, London 1975)

Eno, D. *Pot-pourri from your Garden: How to Make Pot-pourris, Pastilles, Pomanders, Sachets and Herb Pillows* (Juniper Press, Winchester 1978)

Eno, D. *Pressed Flowers* (Juniper Press, Winchester 1980)

Foster, M. *Creating Pictures with Preserved Flowers* (Pelham Books, London 1977)

Hulbert, A. *Victorian Crafts Revived* (Batsford, London 1978)

Jackson, V. *Yesterday's Crafts for Today* (Lutterworth Press, Guildford 1979)

Jeffrey, V. *The Flower Workshop* (Hamlyn, London 1980)

McDowall, P. *Pressed Flower Pictures* (Lutterworth Press, Guildford 1969)

Spry, C. *Encyclopedia of Flower Arranging* (Pan Books, London 1975)

Stevenson, V. *Flowercraft* (Hamlyn, London 1977)

Waring, J. *Early American Stencils on Walls and Furniture* (Dover Publications, New York 1968)

Wilkinson, J. *Flower Fabrications* (Butterick Publishing, New York 1978)

Woods, P. *Flowers from Fabrics* (David & Charles, Newton Abbot 1976)

Wright-Smith, R. *Picture Framing* (Orbis Publishing, London 1980)

Useful addresses

Tools and equipment for general use can be obtained from local hardware, haberdashery or stationary stores. More specialized materials are available from most craft shops and artists' suppliers.

Popular Crafts, 13–35 Bridge Street, Hemel Hempstead, Herts., publishes a *Guide to Good Craft Suppliers*, and the classified sections of most arts and crafts magazines also contain useful addresses. The following list is a small selection of specialist suppliers.

Florist's sundries
Handley Reed and Co. Ltd., 68 Wansey Street, London SE17.
Many florists, such as Longmans, 7 Gees Court, London W1 and branches, will supply small amounts of stub wires and other equipment.

Aromatic oils, dried herbs, pot-pourri mixtures
Aromatic Oil Company, 12 Littlegate Street, Oxford.
Herbs from the Hoo, 46 Church Street, Buckden, St Neots, Cambs.
Oaks Farm House Crafts, Felmingham, North Walsham, Norfolk.
Elizabeth Walker, Meadow Herbs Ltd., Copthall Place, Anna Valley, nr. Andover, Hants.
Woods of Windsor, Queen Charlotte Street, Windsor.

Flower presses, frames, paperweights
Peter Bates, The Mount, Cattishead, Fareham, Hants.
Habitat Designs Ltd., 206 King's Road, SW3 and branches.
Joy Strong, 16 Everlands, Cam, Dursely, Gloucs.

Stencils
A wide selection of stencils and stencil paper is available from Paperchase Products Ltd., 213 Tottenham Court Road, London W1 and 167 Fulham Road, London SW3.
Stencil kits are also available from Lyn le Grice Stencils, Wells Head, Temple Guiting, Cheltenham, Gloucs.

Modelling materials, dyes, general crafts
Arts and Crafts Shop, 194 Union Street, Oldham, Lancs.
Arts and Handicrafts, 18 Station Parade, Harrogate, Yorks.
Cowling and Wilcox Ltd., 26 Broadwick Street, London W1 (mail order service).
Craftsmith, 18 George Street, Richmond, Surrey.
Dryad, Northgates, Leicester LE1 4QR (mail order service).
Handicrafts, New Road, Peterborough, Huntingdonshire.
Hobby Horse, 15–17 Langton Street, London SW10 (mail order service).
Leisure Crafts Centre, 1 Castle Street, Tunbridge Wells, Kent.
Reeves Dryad Ltd., 178 Kensington High Street, London W8 (mail order service)
Winsor & Newton Ltd., 24 Rathbone Place, London W1.

Embroidery threads, canvas etc.
Mary Allen, Wirksworth, Derbyshire.

Beads
Warehouse, 39 Neal Street, London WC2.

Patchwork scraps etc.
Laura Ashley, 35 Bow Street, London WC2 and branches.
Flores, Albion Street, Bury, Lancs.
The Patchwork Dog & The Calico Cat, 21 Chalk Farm Road, London NW1 (templates, stencils etc.).

Leather offcuts
J.T. Batchelor & Co., 146 Fleet Road, NW3 (mail order service).

Picture acknowledgments

The publishers are grateful to the following for their permission to reproduce the photographs:
page 42: Octopus Books; pages 50–1: Lyn le Grice Stencils; pages 74–5: Hamlyn Publishing Group (*The Flower Workshop*).

All other photographs were specially taken for the book by Paul Williams.

Dressing table set (page 39), paper knife (page 43), inkwell and box (page 87) from Pearl Cross Limited, Antique Jewellers, 35 St Martin's Court, London WC2.
Lamp (page 43) from The Lamp Shop, 24 Bedfordbury, London WC2.
Wicker cradle (pages 90–1) from Covent Garden General Store, 111 Long Acre, London WC2.
Pine shelf unit (page 70) and wooden rocking horse (pages 94–5) from Naturally British, 13 New Row, London WC2.
Toys (pages 94–5) from Knutz Limited, 1 Russell Street, London WC2.

Index